Building Self-Worth

A Teen Guide to a Strong Sense of Self, Purpose, and Meaning

By: Jennifer Costanza, MA, LMFT

© Copyright 2023 - All rights reserved.

The content contained within this book may not be reproduced, duplicated or transmitted without direct written permission from the author or the publisher.

Under no circumstances will any blame or legal responsibility be held against the publisher, or author, for any damages, reparation, or monetary loss due to the information contained within this book, either directly or indirectly.

Legal Notice:

This book is copyright protected. It is only for personal use. You cannot amend, distribute, sell, use, quote or paraphrase any part, or the content within this book, without the consent of the Jennifer Costanza MA, LMFT or Rise and Shine Publishing.

Disclaimer Notice:

Please note the information contained within this document is for educational and entertainment purposes only. All effort has been executed to present accurate, up to date, reliable, complete information. No warranties of any kind are declared or implied. Readers acknowledge that the author is not engaged in the rendering of legal, financial, medical or professional advice. The content within this book has been derived from various sources. Please consult a licensed professional before attempting any techniques outlined in this book.

By reading this document, the reader agrees that under no circumstances is the author responsible for any losses, direct or indirect, that are incurred as a result of the use of the information contained within this document, including, but not limited to, errors, omissions, or inaccuracies.

Table of Contents

TABLE OF CONTENTS

TABLE OF CONTENTS 5

INTRODUCTION 1

    STEPPING STONES: YOUR PATHWAY TO SELF-WORTH 2

CHAPTER 1: BUILDING SELF-ESTEEM 5

    WHAT IS SELF-WORTH AND HOW IS IT RELATED TO SELF-ESTEEM? 6
    WHY IS GOOD SELF-ESTEEM IMPORTANT? 7
        Mental and Emotional Well-Being 7
        Knowing Yourself and Your Needs 8
        Ability to Believe in Yourself 8
        Being on the Learning Curve 9
        Resourcefulness 10
        Flexibility and Openness 11
        Assertiveness in Decision-Making 11
        Healthy Relationships 12
        Life Balance 12
    WHAT ARE THE EFFECTS OF LOW SELF-ESTEEM? 13
        Causes 13
        Effects 14
    HOW CAN I BUILD MY SELF-ESTEEM? 20
    EXERCISE: SELF-ESTEEM JOURNALING 22

CHAPTER 2: DISCOVERING MY IDENTITY 23

    WHAT ARE MY CORE VALUES AND BELIEFS? 24
    WHAT MAKES ME UNIQUE AND WHY IS THIS IMPORTANT? 25
    HOW CAN I ESTABLISH MY IDENTITY? 27
        Practice Self-Reflection 28
        Explore New Perspectives 28
        Welcome Constructive Criticisms 29
        Seek Personal Growth 30
        Embrace Imperfections and Self-Acceptance 30
        Pushing Beyond Your Comfort Zone 31
    EXERCISE: IDENTITY MAPPING EXERCISE 32

CHAPTER 3: FINDING PURPOSE AND MEANING 34

    What Are My Strengths and Areas of Improvement? 34
    What Are My Interests? 35
    What Are My Passions? 36
    What Is Important to Me? 37
    What or Who Inspires Me? 38
    What Kind of Future Do I Envision For Myself? 39

  What Kind of Change Do I Want to See in the World? 39
  How Can I Make a Positive Impact? 41
 Exercise: Self Reflection 41

CHAPTER 4: MAKING MEANINGFUL RELATIONSHIPS TO BOOST SELF-ESTEEM .44

 What Obstacles Come in the Way of Relationships? 45
  Low Confidence 46
  Poor Communication 46
  Social Media 47
  Competition 48
  Manipulation 49
 What Interpersonal Skills Do I Need? 50
  Communication Skills 51
  Depth 52
  Empathy 52
  Vulnerability and Honesty 53
  Conflict Resolution 54
  Trust 54
  Confidence 55
 Why Are Connections Important? 56
  Maintaining Healthy Vulnerability 57
  Family 58
  Friendships 59
  Other Relationships 60
 Exercise: Connect the Dots 61

CHAPTER 5: OVERCOMING COMMON CHALLENGES 64

 What Are Common Challenges That Teenagers Like Me Face? 65
  Mental Health Issues 65
  Peer Pressure 66
  Bullying 67
  Social Media 67
  Risky Behaviors and Addictions 69
  Academic Pressures 70
 How Do I Overcome Challenges in My Teenhood? 70
  Guidance or Counseling 71
  Support and Community 72
  Self-Care 73
  Patience 73
  Honesty With Oneself 74
  Courage 75

    Exercise: Drawing Out Your Bravery 76
CHAPTER 6: SUCCEEDING IN SCHOOL AND BEYOND 78
    How Do I Find Fulfillment? 78
        Find Motivation 79
        Deal With Anxiety 80
        Understand Your Personality 82
        Manage Stress and Fatigue 83
        Minimize Distractions 84
        Eliminate Apathy and Find Direction 85
        Drop Unhealthy Comparisons 87
    How Do I Become the Person I Want to Be? 88
        Discover What Drives You 89
        Understand Your Relationship With Money 90
        Find Interests and Passions 91
        Set Clear Goals 92
        Improve Time Management Skills 93
        Learn to Say No 94
        Develop and Pursue Healthy Daily Habits 95
        Develop Systems for Studying and Learning 96
        Tenacity and Persistence 97
        Recognize That Life Has Seasons 98
    Succeeding in School and Beyond—A Comprehensive Approach 99
CONCLUSION 103
REFERENCES 105

Introduction

Looking back on my teenage years, it's akin to revisiting an intense, vivid movie, a mixture of feelings, experiences, and life lessons. Back then, I was a young person on a journey, searching for my own identity and value.

Hi, I'm Jennifer Costanza, a licensed marriage and family therapist. The highlights of my adolescence were marked by freedom and exploration. I reveled in the first tastes of autonomy, the excitement of new experiences, and the thrill of knowledge. Every scientific experiment was an adventure, every teamwork experience was a lesson in unity, and the rollercoaster of first love and heartbreak taught me the delicate dance between joy and sorrow.

However, adolescence isn't all sunshine and rainbows. I grappled with the pressures of my peers, the rigors of school, and the constant need to belong while yearning to stand out. Navigating these challenges, alongside dealing with body image concerns and the influence of societal expectations, frequently spiraled into a vortex of self-doubt and anxiety. For over nearly two decades, I've devoted myself to working with people from all walks of life, gaining a deep understanding of their battles with self-esteem.

The obstacles in my path didn't deter me; instead, they ignited a spark within me. They pushed me toward a field that allowed me to unravel the intricate workings of the human mind and its remarkable resilience. My personal journey has driven me to write this book, an endeavor to help young individuals foster a strong sense of self-worth that can weather life's many storms.

I've spent the better part of 17 years working with individuals of all ages, gaining insights into their struggles with self-worth. I've learned their stories, empathized with their battles, and have been privileged to witness their metamorphosis. My foundation in neuroscience and biopsychology equips me with a unique lens to observe how the mind and body influence our perception of self.

In my role as a therapist, with a focus on trauma and anxiety disorders, I've witnessed how deeply self-worth influences our mental health struggles. This fundamental aspect of our mindset, particularly critical during the formative years of childhood and adolescence, serves as the cornerstone of our emotional stability. This book represents the synthesis of my professional journey and my firm belief in our innate capacity for transformation. It's my hope that it will guide teenagers and those around them in nurturing a strong sense of self-worth. It's time to place self-worth at the heart of our dialogue about mental health and emotional well-being. Let's equip you with the tools you need to build a solid sense of self that originates from within and remains unfazed by external factors.

Welcome to a transformative journey that I hope will enable you to construct resilient self-worth that endures. Let's begin this exploration together.

Stepping Stones: Your Pathway to Self-Worth

In this transformative journey, I hope to reach out to the vibrant and incredibly valuable community of teenagers. I want to talk to you about how you can build and nurture your self-worth, the keystone of confidence and self-esteem. This manuscript is more than just a collection of theories and observations; it is an actionable guide that will walk you through the tumultuous waves of adolescence and lead you toward finding purpose and meaning in your journey to adulthood.

I believe that self-worth is not simply about feeling good about yourself; it's about recognizing and appreciating your inherent value. As you leaf through the pages of this book, you'll find practical steps and strategies that will guide you toward becoming more comfortable and confident in your own skin. It's about acknowledging and embracing your individuality, quirks, and strengths and turning the awkwardness and unease of teen years into a celebration of self-discovery and growth.

Life as a teenager is often a whirlwind of experiences. You'll face many challenges: fluctuating friendships, the cruel presence of bullying, the quest to fit in, the struggle to assert your individuality, the academic pressures, and the constant battle with self-doubt and insecurity. While these challenges may seem overwhelming, remember this: They are part of your journey, and you can learn to navigate them with grace and resilience.

This book is your guide to understanding, managing, and growing through these challenges. The chapters will be your companions, helping you understand and answer some of the most pressing questions you may have. "How can I be more confident as a young person?" "How do I deal with common challenges that come with adolescence?" and "How do I establish my identity and find my purpose and meaning?"

Through the pages of this book, I aim to answer these questions and more. Each chapter is designed to provide you with insights, strategies, and techniques that are rooted in years of practice and research. They will help you become your own strongest advocate, capable of loving and accepting yourself as you are while continually growing and evolving.

There's an old saying that rings true: "Life isn't about finding yourself; it's about creating yourself." This book is your guide in this creation process. It will help you understand that the only person you need to please and impress is the one you see in the mirror. It will guide you toward recognizing your self-worth and teach you never to let anyone or anything make you feel otherwise.

Remember, the journey of adolescence isn't about being perfect; it's about being *you*. It's about acknowledging your worth, embracing your potential, and becoming the person *you* aspire to be. This book is my hand extended to you, welcoming you into a world of self-discovery, self-acceptance, and self-love.

So, gear up for an incredible journey, a journey to your true self. This is your story of growth, resilience, and empowerment. I'm thrilled to be your guide and companion in this crucial journey toward understanding and enhancing your self-worth. Let's take this path together, one step at a time.

Welcome aboard to an empowering journey of self-worth, self-love, and self-discovery.

Remember, you are enough, you always were, and you always will be.

Chapter 1:

Building Self-esteem

Self-worth comes from one thing—thinking that you are worthy. –Wayne Dyer

Have you ever thought about how much power we hold within ourselves? Our self-esteem acts like an internal compass, pointing toward our worth and value, always whispering, "I am enough," "I matter," and "I am capable."

Several years into my practice, I remember crossing paths with a young woman, let's call her Clara. Energetic, eloquent, and exceptionally gifted, Clara was a spark of joy in any setting. Yet, beneath this lively facade, Clara was silently wrestling with self-doubt and fragile self-esteem. Despite being a high achiever, she attributed her successes to luck, brushing off compliments as if they were meant for someone else.

Unfortunately, Clara's struggle isn't an isolated case. It echoes in the lives of many who question their worthiness. So, this chapter is for every "Clara" out there; to shed light on the path to bolstering self-esteem and understanding its intricate link with self-worth.

We will first unpack the definitions of self-worth and self-esteem and comprehend their deep-seated connection. We'll explore why robust self-esteem isn't merely desirable but essential for our mental and emotional health. High self-esteem provides a clearer lens to understand ourselves and our needs, fosters our faith in our abilities, keeps us on a continuous learning path, and enhances resourcefulness.

It promotes flexibility, decisiveness, enriches our relationships, and brings balance to our lives. However, we will also look at the shadow side, the potential fallout of low self-esteem. We'll investigate its root causes, impacts, and how it undermines our sense of self-worth.

Be it perfectionism, excessive self-criticism, fear, anxiety, depression, engaging in high-risk activities, or strained relationships, these are all potential offshoots of low self-esteem. Recognizing these impacts underscores the importance of nurturing our self-esteem.

Toward the end of this chapter, you will find actionable steps to grow and foster your self-esteem. Similar to a gardener tending to their plants, self-esteem requires diligent care, patience, and love. Self-esteem is not about morphing into a different person; it's about evolving into our best self. Self-esteem isn't about changing who we fundamentally are; rather, it's about blossoming into the best version of ourselves. As we journey through this chapter side by side, my objective is to arm you with the necessary resources to nurture a resilient, affirmative self-esteem.

What Is Self-Worth and How Is It Related to Self-Esteem?

Self-worth and self-esteem, often used interchangeably, are two distinct yet intricately connected facets of our psychological makeup.

Self-esteem, as defined by Rosenberg (1965), refers to a person's overall subjective emotional evaluation of their own worth. It is a judgment of oneself as well as an attitude toward oneself. Factors that influence self-esteem can range from childhood experiences (Orth et al., 2012), achievements or failures (Crocker & Wolfe, 2001), societal and peer expectations (Leary et al., 1995), to our body image (Grogan, 2008) and how we perceive others to view us (Cooley, 1902).

On the other hand, self-worth is a more fundamental sense of value or lovability, a belief in our inherent worthiness as human beings. It is not contingent upon our accomplishments, societal status, or what others think of us but comes from within (Neff, 2003).

The relationship between self-worth and self-esteem is profoundly intertwined. Self-esteem is often seen as the manifestation of our self-worth. When we have a strong sense of self-worth, we're likely to have healthier self-esteem (Neff, 2003). Conversely, if we base our self-esteem on external factors, our self-worth can be extremely volatile.

Our self-worth impacts our self-esteem by serving as the foundation on which self-esteem is built. If we believe in our inherent value (high self-worth), then even if we fail or face rejection, our self-esteem can remain intact (Baumeister et al., 2003). On the other hand, self-esteem can impact our self-worth by reinforcing or diminishing our fundamental sense of value. When we experience success or positive reinforcement (high self-esteem), it can affirm our self-worth. However, if we constantly devalue ourselves (low self-esteem), it can undermine our core belief in our worthiness (Harter, 1999).

Why Is Good Self-Esteem Important?

Having strong self-esteem plays a crucial role in our overall well-being, shaping our mental health, our relationships, and our ability to navigate life's challenges (Orth et al., 2012). Positive self-esteem acts as a buffer against mental health issues like depression and anxiety (Orth & Robins, 2013). Take, for instance, Jamie, a teenager I worked with, who, despite a significant sports injury, maintained his emotional balance. People with high self-esteem are often more in tune with their needs, desires, and boundaries (Branden, 1994). There are other important reasons why good self-esteem is important.

Mental and Emotional Well-Being

Promoting mental and emotional well-being is an integral part of enhancing your self-esteem. When you value yourself, it paves the way to a higher functioning and a more fulfilling life.

First, recognizing your self-worth aids you in actualizing your potential. When you genuinely value who you are, it encourages you to align your actions with your authentic self, leading to a sense of fulfillment. Just as Maslow's Hierarchy of Needs suggests, achieving self-actualization, becoming the best version of yourself, often requires you to have a solid foundation of self-esteem (Maslow, 1943).

Furthermore, valuing your worth aids you in maintaining a positive outlook on life, allowing you to manage your emotions effectively. When you hold yourself in high regard, you're less likely to get trapped in negative thoughts, leading to better emotional well-being. This does not mean that you won't face emotional challenges. Instead, it suggests that with good self-esteem, you'll be better equipped to handle these challenges.

In a nutshell, understanding and valuing your worth can significantly enhance your mental and emotional well-being, enabling you to function at a higher level and actualize your potential.

Knowing Yourself and Your Needs

Developing an understanding of your identity is a significant aspect of bolstering your self-esteem and self-worth. Identity refers to your understanding of who you are, encompassing your values, beliefs, and aspirations. As you come to know yourself better, you will be able to better meet your needs.

By taking the time to reflect on and understand your identity, you can pinpoint your strengths and weaknesses, likes and dislikes, passions, and personal values. This self-awareness plays a crucial role in nurturing your self-esteem because it fosters acceptance of who you are. You become more comfortable in your skin and, in turn, value yourself more. This has been repeatedly demonstrated in research, indicating that self-understanding and identity are foundational to healthy self-esteem (Schwartz et al., 2005).

Furthermore, a clear understanding of your identity will also help you to understand your needs better. Recognizing your needs is critical for maintaining your well-being and promoting your self-esteem. By acknowledging and respecting your needs, whether they're emotional, physical, or social, you convey to yourself that you are worth caring for.

The journey to understanding yourself and your needs, your identity, can be deeply rewarding and integral to fostering your self-esteem.

Ability to Believe in Yourself

Believing in oneself is a core component of self-esteem; it's about having confidence in your abilities and trusting in your judgment. When you believe in yourself, you free yourself from barriers that may be holding you back.

Releasing barriers can take many forms. These barriers might be internal, such as self-doubt, fear of failure, or negative self-talk. Or they might be external, like critical comments from others or societal norms. Recognizing and challenging these barriers are crucial steps toward boosting your self-esteem (Bandura, 1997).

When you start believing in your abilities, you no longer let these barriers dictate your actions. For instance, if you fear failure, you might be hesitant to take on new challenges. But when you believe in yourself, you begin to see failure not as a pitfall but as a learning opportunity.

The more you believe in yourself, the more likely you are to set and pursue ambitious goals, further enhancing your self-esteem. Research has shown that individuals who have a higher belief in their capabilities often set more challenging goals and are more committed to achieving them (Locke et al., 1984).

Developing the ability to believe in yourself and to release the barriers standing in your way are powerful ways to nurture your self-esteem and expand your horizons.

Being on the Learning Curve

Life is a continuous learning process. Each new experience, encounter, and situation provides an opportunity to learn, grow, and shape your self-esteem. Being on this learning curve implies that you are open to new experiences and are willing to learn from them, building resilience and confidence along the way.

Resilience refers to the capacity to recover quickly from difficulties and adapt well in the face of adversity. As you navigate the ups and downs of life, your ability to bounce back from setbacks will play a significant role in shaping your self-esteem (Masten, 2001). For instance, failure might initially dampen your self-esteem. But by embracing the learning curve and viewing failure as a learning opportunity, you can foster resilience and strengthen your self-esteem.

Each success and failure on your learning journey contributes to your confidence. Confidence, in essence, is a belief in your abilities. When you learn from your experiences, you're not just accumulating knowledge or skills; you're also gaining confidence in your ability to navigate future situations. This self-confidence further bolsters your self-esteem (Kaplan & Maehr, 1999).

Being on the learning curve and cultivating resilience and confidence is a continuous process that can significantly enhance your self-esteem.

Resourcefulness

Your ability to be resourceful is a critical component that bolsters your sense of self-worth. Think of resourcefulness as being able to navigate a ship through stormy seas—finding the right paths, using the winds to your advantage, and overcoming hurdles with agility and creativity. It's about thriving in adversity, not just surviving.

When you flex your resourcefulness muscle, you find that it's not just about problem-solving. It's about using the tools at your disposal, both internal and external, to the fullest extent. And in doing so, you amplify your confidence and competence, key elements that elevate your self-esteem.

Bandura's theory on self-efficacy points to this dynamic. It suggests that when you believe you can overcome challenges and that you're resourceful, this perception triggers an upward spiral of self-esteem (Bandura, 1997).

Being resourceful also involves adopting a solution-focused mindset. It's about owning your life's narrative and taking the driver's seat in your journey. This sense of agency instills a powerful sense of control, reaffirming your capabilities and bolstering your belief that you can positively shape your life's path.

More importantly, resourcefulness paves the way for thriving. Thriving isn't just about growth; it's about persisting even when the going gets tough. When you flex your resourcefulness, you don't just seek survival; you aim for growth and positive transformation. This sense of flourishing provides a substantial boost to your self-esteem, nurturing your overall sense of self-worth (Carver, 1998).

Being resourceful is like carrying a magic toolbox; it equips you with the confidence to face life's challenges, enriches your self-esteem, and enables you to thrive amidst life's ups and downs.

Flexibility and Openness

Human beings are continually changing. To thrive amidst this constant flux, we need two allies by our side: flexibility and openness. Both are qualities that not only help us navigate life's ebb and flow but also significantly build and support our self-esteem.

When we speak of flexibility, we're referring to our adaptability, our readiness to pivot when life takes unexpected turns. The more we cultivate this attribute, the more adept we become at handling life's surprises. Our confidence in tackling unforeseen circumstances grows, fortifying our self-esteem in the process (Martin et al., 2012).

Openness, however, plays a different, yet equally crucial, role. It's about welcoming new ideas, embracing diversity, and being ready for novelty. As we expose ourselves to various perspectives and experiences, we broaden our understanding of the world. This expanded worldview fosters personal growth, which in turn elevates our self-esteem. Moreover, openness nurtures empathy, enhancing our social relationships and adding another layer of strength to our self-esteem (McCrae & Costa, 1987).

Assertiveness in Decision-Making

Assertiveness is a critical component of decision-making and, consequently, in the evolution of our self-esteem. Assertiveness encourages us to advocate for ourselves, letting our voices reverberate, all while respecting the viewpoints of others around us (Ames et al., 2017).

Those who embrace assertiveness tend to make choices that resonate with their intrinsic values and personal needs rather than conform to external pressures or the persuasive voices of others. When assertiveness and decision come together, a sense of authenticity and autonomy occurs, which, in turn, cultivates a more robust sense of self-esteem (Heppner & Heppner, 2004).

Also, assertiveness serves as a catalyst for open dialogue and reciprocal respect in our relationships. This translates into more rewarding interactions and fosters a nurturing social environment. The positive result further amplifies self-esteem as individuals feel acknowledged and valued (Lange & Jakubowski, 1976).

Infusing assertiveness into our decision-making processes provides a considerable uplift to our self-esteem. By steadfastly upholding our decisions and principles, we enhance our contentment, authenticity, and autonomy, all of which powerfully reinforce our self-esteem and self-worth.

Healthy Relationships

Healthy relationships can play a significant role in nurturing and reinforcing our self-esteem. They provide an environment of mutual respect, empathy, understanding, and genuine love, all factors that can bolster our feelings of self-worth and acceptance (Reis et al., 2000).

When we share a bond with someone who acknowledges and values our unique qualities, it can tremendously elevate our self-esteem. Engaging with those we have solid, healthy relationships allows us to view ourselves from a place of appreciation. This nurtures self-love and self-acceptance within us. Consistently receiving such affirmations can progressively steer our self-perception toward a brighter, more positive stance (Murray et al., 2006).

Healthy relationships allow for open communication, allowing us to express our thoughts, feelings, and desires without fear of judgment or rejection. This level of understanding and acceptance strengthens our belief in our worth and enhances our self-esteem (Pierce et al., 1996).

On the flip side, relationships marred by disrespect, manipulation, or lack of support can contribute to lower self-esteem. Consequently, it's crucial to surround ourselves with relationships that uplift us and contribute positively to our self-image.

Life Balance

A well-balanced life is often seen as an indication of healthy self-esteem. It's about finding the equilibrium between our personal and professional lives, our physical health and mental well-being, and our time for ourselves and others (Srivastava & Kumar, 2017).

When we have a balanced life, we are better equipped to handle stress and challenges and less likely to burn out. This sense of balance also provides a firm foundation for self-esteem. Knowing that we are effectively managing different aspects of our lives gives us a sense of control and accomplishment (Kumar & Mishra, 2011).

A high level of self-esteem can make it easier to maintain this balance. We are more likely to take time for self-care, set boundaries, and prioritize tasks in a way that suits our needs and capacities. In turn, having a balanced life can boost our self-esteem. When we see that we are capable of managing our responsibilities and making time for things we enjoy, our confidence in our abilities grows (Neff, 2011).

However, it's crucial to remember that a balanced life doesn't mean achieving perfection in all areas. It's about recognizing our limits, setting realistic expectations, and giving ourselves permission to rest and recharge.

What Are the Effects of Low Self-Esteem?

In our journey toward understanding self-esteem, it is crucial that we address not only its benefits but also the potential repercussions of a deficient self-image. Low self-esteem can cast a long shadow over various aspects of our lives. It is a sneaky presence, creeping into our thoughts, shaping our perceptions, and influencing our actions, often without us even realizing it.

Understanding the effects of low self-esteem is not merely about identifying the problems but is a necessary step toward healing. As we illuminate these issues, we're essentially mapping the terrain of a landscape that can often feel puzzling, arming ourselves with the knowledge we need to navigate toward healthier self-esteem.

Causes

Low self-esteem is often the byproduct of a variety of intricate factors and life experiences that gradually shape how we see ourselves. Let's look deeper into these influences, starting with the role of our early home life. The impressions of childhood are lasting, and for children who navigate an unstable home environment or experience neglectful or abusive parenting, the impacts can be profound. Insecurity and feelings of inadequacy can stem from these experiences, imprinting on the child's developing identity and persisting into adulthood (Trzesniewski et al., 2006).

Next, consider the influence of a family member grappling with substance addiction, such as alcoholism. This situation can cultivate an environment of instability and unpredictability, leading to heightened anxiety and lower self-esteem. The inconsistency and lack of security can be particularly damaging to children in their formative years (Anda et al., 2002).

Bullying, another significant factor contributing to low self-esteem, can manifest in various forms at school, online, or elsewhere. Experiencing persistent humiliation, exclusion, or aggression can push individuals into believing they are unworthy of respect or kindness, thereby reinforcing a negative self-image (Reijntjes et al., 2010).

Individuals with physical disabilities may also struggle with self-esteem. Societal stigma and discrimination can impose significant emotional burdens. Negative societal attitudes toward disabilities can be internalized, resulting in feelings of inadequacy or worthlessness (Nosek et al., 2003).

Lastly, undiagnosed or untreated mental health conditions, such as depression, anxiety, or ADHD, can exacerbate low self-esteem. These disorders often come with symptomatic negative self-perception and self-criticism, which can further degrade an individual's self-esteem (Sowislo & Orth, 2013).

In our journey toward self-esteem improvement, understanding these root causes is instrumental. With this knowledge at our disposal, we can address these issues more effectively, enabling a path to enhanced self-worth and confidence.

Effects

The effects of low self-esteem can extend deeply into an individual's life, affecting their mental, emotional, and social well-being. This issue often gives rise to more pronounced mental health struggles as a pattern of negative self-thinking sets in. The ensuing feelings of worthlessness can subsequently pave the way for conditions like depression and anxiety (Orth et al., 2009).

Having low self-esteem is like carrying around a heavy weight that impacts almost every area of your life. It's like seeing yourself through a distorted lens, where your sense of self-worth takes a hit. You find yourself chasing the elusive ghost of perfection, only to feel downcast when the mark is missed. It's a cycle, really. You nitpick at your shortcomings, blowing even the tiniest of mistakes way out of proportion.

This clouded vision of yourself often goes hand-in-hand with feelings of overwhelming fear, bouts of anxiety, and a lingering gloom of depression. Afraid of failure, you might steer clear of new experiences or become gripped by worries about the "what ifs" of the future. In darker moments, some might even turn to reckless behaviors, hoping to escape or numb the pain, whether it's through substances or other harmful activities.

And it's not just an internal battle. Your relationships can take a hit too. Trust becomes a rare commodity, whether it's doubting your decisions or questioning the motives of those around you. You might stick around in unhealthy relationships longer than you should, thinking you can't do any better. Or, on the flip side, you might put up walls, misreading innocent comments as criticisms. Navigating this rough terrain isn't easy, but it underscores the need to reach out, lean on others, and sometimes even seek professional help to rebuild that lost self-confidence.

Low self-esteem often roots itself in our earlier years, shaped by challenging experiences or perhaps the absence of positive reinforcement. As we navigate life, societal pressures, coupled with the relentless world of social media, can exacerbate these feelings of unworthiness. It becomes all too easy to fall into the comparison trap, gauging our worth by looking sideways. However, it's essential to remember that we all have unique paths and timelines. Overcoming these feelings takes conscious effort, emphasizing self-love and self-acceptance. Surrounding ourselves with nurturing individuals and spaces can help change the narrative we have about ourselves, leading us toward a more wholesome and self-affirming outlook.

Low self-esteem's impact is far-reaching, influencing not just the way individuals view themselves but also how they engage with the world around them. Understanding these effects is critical to devising effective strategies that foster better self-esteem and promote healthier ways of interacting with oneself and others.

Perfectionism

Perfectionism often emerges as a consequence of low self-esteem, acting as a demanding drive to accomplish unnaturally high objectives. Those who identify as perfectionists typically see anything less than perfect as an indication of failure, with minor mishaps causing substantial stress and self-disapproval (Flett et al., 2002).

A lack of self-esteem can further instigate this tendency toward perfectionism. Individuals grappling with self-worth may feel that they can only be valued or cherished if they are infallible. As a result, they set incredibly high benchmarks for themselves, sure that achieving these formidable goals is the only path to asserting their worthiness (Frost et al., 1990).

Nonetheless, the unattainable nature of these goals often results in a continuous feeling of insufficiency, thereby compounding low self-esteem. This unyielding cycle of diminished self-esteem and perfectionism can cultivate a continuous feedback loop of self-rebuke and dissatisfaction. Self-worth becomes tethered to performance, leaving self-esteem precarious and fluctuating (Hewitt et al., 2003).

Recognizing this association between low self-esteem and perfectionism is integral to dismantling the cycle. Cultivating a sense of self-kindness, accepting oneself as is, and learning to set achievable goals can help alleviate the repercussions of perfectionism, paving the way for a healthier level of self-worth.

Hypercritical Self-Perception

Individuals grappling with low self-esteem often entertain an overly critical perception of themselves. They are inclined to fixate on their shortcomings, undermining or even disregarding their strengths and achievements, as if scrutinizing their identity through a misshapen lens. This skewed viewpoint highlights the negatives, while the positives seem to dissipate into the background (Rüsch et al., 2007).

Such self-evaluation engenders an imbalanced and diminished self-image. A mere blunder might be perceived as a catastrophic failure, precipitating severe self-reproach. It's common for these individuals to place undue blame on themselves for setbacks that are beyond their control, spiraling into feelings of guilt and shame and further eroding their sense of self-worth (Orth et al., 2008).

This persistent thinking can set the stage for a self-fulfilling prophecy. When individuals restrict themselves from taking risks or pursuing opportunities due to a fear of failure, they inadvertently fortify their feelings of incompetence (Baumeister et al., 2003).

Interrupting this negative self-perception becomes a pivotal stride in enhancing self-esteem. Strategies such as cognitive restructuring, embracing self-compassion, and practicing mindfulness have demonstrated efficacy in mitigating such adverse self-assessments and fostering a more balanced and realistic self-view (Neff & Vonk, 2009).

Fear, Anxiety, and Depression

Low self-esteem often serves as fertile ground for the growth of fear, anxiety, and even depression. Living with low self-esteem might mean living in constant apprehension of rejection or failure, leading to a state of perpetual anxiety (Sowislo & Orth, 2013). Overthinking past slip-ups or possible future pitfalls can induce a persistent condition of worry and distress, leaving a person mentally and physically drained.

Furthermore, low self-esteem can pave the way for the onset of depression. People who grapple with feelings of self-worth often face a sense of desolation, alienation, or the belief that they're unlovable, all of which are symptoms closely associated with depression (Orth et al., 2009). They may find it hard to enjoy their favorite pastimes or sustain relationships because they feel worthless. The fragile state of self-esteem can also mean they're less resilient to life's adversities, making them more susceptible to depressive phases.

Understanding the intricate connection between low self-esteem and these mental health conditions is essential. Strengthening self-esteem isn't the ultimate solution to fear, anxiety, or depression, but it is an instrumental part of managing these issues. Enhancing self-esteem provides a solid base to deal with life's stresses, lessens the intensity of anxiety and depressive symptoms, and enhances the overall mental health quality (Sowislo & Orth, 2013).

Risky Behaviors

Low self-esteem can sometimes push individuals toward adopting risky behaviors, acting as a catalyst for potentially harmful decisions and actions. A distorted self-image, where one perceives oneself in a negative light, may lead to a tendency to engage in activities that are damaging, both physically and emotionally. Such behavior can be a misplaced attempt to validate oneself or escape feelings of inadequacy and low self-worth (McGee & Williams, 2000).

In adolescents and young adults, low self-esteem is often associated with higher susceptibility to substance abuse, reckless driving, or unsafe sexual behavior (Donnellan et al., 2005). This trend can be attributed to the quest for immediate gratification or the urge to feel "accepted" and "valued" in peer groups. The transient pleasure or validation obtained from these actions often masks the underlying issue of low self-esteem.

In adults, low self-esteem could manifest in risky behaviors such as excessive drinking, gambling, or staying in abusive relationships (Trzesniewski et al., 2006). These behaviors can stem from a distorted self-perception and a belief that one is undeserving of better experiences or healthier relationships.

Understanding the connection between low self-esteem and risky behaviors is crucial for intervention. By strengthening self-esteem, individuals can gain better control over their actions, make healthier decisions, and reduce the propensity for risky behavior.

Relationship Problems

Low self-esteem can substantially impact the quality and longevity of relationships. It often triggers behaviors and patterns that can create issues within the relational dynamics, impacting one's connection with friends, family, and romantic partners.

Individuals with low self-esteem often struggle with feelings of unworthiness, leading them to question their value within a relationship. They may experience constant fear of rejection or abandonment, which can manifest as clinginess or excessive dependence on their partner (Murray et al., 2001). This fear may also manifest in the opposite way, pushing them to distance themselves to avoid potential heartbreak.

Moreover, people with low self-esteem may interpret the neutral or even positive actions of their partners through a lens of negativity. They might perceive innocent comments as criticism or misinterpret affectionate gestures as pity or obligation, causing unnecessary conflict (Murray et al., 2001). This negative bias in interpretations can lead to constant misunderstandings and disagreements.

Low self-esteem can also contribute to a pattern of unhealthy relationships. Individuals may settle for relationships where they are neglected, disrespected, or abused, believing they do not deserve better. They may have difficulty standing up for themselves and setting boundaries, leading to one-sided relationships that further damage their self-esteem (Downey et al., 1998).

Addressing self-esteem is thus a crucial step toward improving relationship quality. By fostering a healthier sense of self-worth, individuals can navigate their relationships with more confidence, understanding, and mutual respect.

How Can I Build My Self-Esteem?

Building up your self-esteem is an insightful and transformative journey of understanding and embracing oneself. Start with self-reflection and becoming more self-aware. Gain a deeper understanding of who you are, recognizing your strengths, talents, and accomplishments while also acknowledging your weaknesses and areas for growth. Everyone has unique gifts and areas they can work on. By accepting both, you begin to appreciate your intrinsic value (Roberts & Monroe, 1992).

Remember that your internal dialogue significantly influences your self-esteem. Embrace positive affirmations and self-talk, using them to reinforce your sense of self-worth. Make a conscious effort to replace any negative self-perceptions with positive ones. Encourage yourself in the same way you would support a close friend, offering kindness and understanding instead of criticism (Mann et al., 2004).

As part of your self-esteem journey, it's important to set realistic goals. These targets provide direction and purpose, and the process of striving toward them can boost your self-confidence. When you achieve these goals, take time to acknowledge your success. Celebrating achievements, big or small, plays a crucial role in building your self-esteem (Bandura, 1986).

Taking care of yourself is essential when it comes to nurturing your self-esteem. Engage in activities that make you feel good about yourself, such as exercise for physical wellness, reading or learning something new for mental stimulation, or spending time with loved ones for emotional health. Mindfulness and meditation practices can also help cultivate a positive self-perception and overall well-being (Neff, 2003).

Your social environment also significantly impacts your self-esteem. Ensure you surround yourself with positive, supportive people who appreciate your worth and help you acknowledge it as well (Rubin et al., 2004).

If you find your self-esteem is persistently low and impacts your daily life, consider seeking help from a mental health professional. Therapies such as Cognitive Behavioral Therapy (CBT) can provide effective strategies to improve your self-esteem (Beck, 2011).

Building self-esteem is not an overnight process; it's a gradual and ongoing journey. However, by investing time, patience, and effort in nurturing your self-worth, you are choosing a path leading toward a healthier, more fulfilled life. The next chapters of this book will provide helpful strategies and support to aid you on your journey.

Exercise: Self-Esteem Journaling

You'll need a notebook and a pen for this exercise. Every day for the next month, dedicate a few minutes to write in your journal. Here are the prompts to consider each day:

Daily affirmation: Start each entry by writing a positive affirmation about yourself. It could be about a personal strength, a recent accomplishment, or a goal you're working toward. The idea is to reframe your thoughts and focus on the positives.

Gratitude: List one or two things that you are grateful for each day. Practicing gratitude has been shown to increase feelings of self-worth and happiness.

Personal reflection: Reflect on one event from your day where you felt good about yourself or learned something about your personal growth. Analyze this event and describe what it taught you about yourself.

Future goals: Write about one small, achievable goal you have for the next day. It could be something as simple as speaking up in a meeting, finishing a chapter of a book, or trying a new hobby. The idea is to set attainable goals and, upon achieving them, acknowledge your abilities and build confidence.

Self-compassion reminder: End your journaling session by writing a statement of self-compassion. This could be something like, "I am a work in progress, and that's okay," or "I am enough just as I am." These reminders help to cultivate self-compassion, a crucial element in enhancing self-esteem (Neff, 2003).

Remember, there's no right or wrong way to journal. This exercise is just for you, so be honest and kind to yourself. Over time, you may find that this exercise helps to boost your self-esteem and overall well-being.

Chapter 2:

Discovering My Identity

There is only one you for all time. Fearlessly be yourself. –Anthony Rapp

In the bustling streets of New York, a small stand-up comedy club tucked away in Greenwich Village hosted an amateur night. This was the stage where a young woman named Sarah found herself one evening, heart pounding with a mix of fear and exhilaration. Sarah, by all means, was an introvert and had never been fond of being the center of attention. Yet, she had a knack for storytelling and a witty sense of humor that could make anyone chuckle.

As she looked at the expectant audience from the stage, she felt a wave of self-doubt. She thought of the professional comedians with their polished acts and wondered if she was making a fool of herself. Maybe she should've stuck with writing, a path that felt safe and comfortable. But then, she remembered why she was there in the first place. It wasn't about being perfect or impressing everyone; it was about expressing her unique perspective on life, embracing her quirks, and sharing her love for humor.

With that thought, she stepped up to the microphone and began her act, channeling her unique charm and wit. She was met with generous laughter and applause. Even when a joke didn't land, she used her quick wit to salvage the situation, and the crowd loved her authenticity.

Sarah's story is an example of the journey of discovering one's identity. She wasn't there to be like other comedians; she was there to be herself. And in doing so, she not only found her unique voice but also learned to celebrate it. In the same way, this chapter encourages you to delve deeper into your own journey of self-discovery and, in the process, learn to appreciate your unique identity.

In all of us, there's a continuous, evolving narrative, a story that defines who we are. It is a combination of our experiences, beliefs, values, desires, and dreams. This narrative, this personal story, is our identity. It's our inner compass guiding our decisions, molding our perspective, and shaping our life's journey.

As we step into the second chapter of our journey, we delve into the profound process of discovering and embracing our unique identity. This chapter is not about creating an artificial facade or attempting to fit into any societal mold, but it's about truly understanding the depth and breadth of our individuality. It's about celebrating what makes us unique, our quirks, strengths, ambitions, and even our shortcomings.

Together, we'll explore our core values and beliefs, understanding how they shape our thoughts, behavior, and interactions. We'll examine the importance of our unique characteristics, discovering the beauty and strength that resides in our individuality. We'll traverse the path of identity establishment, unearthing strategies that will aid us in this process.

We'll learn to practice self-reflection, looking inwards to understand our thoughts, feelings, and motivations better. We'll open our minds to new perspectives, enriching our understanding of the world and our place in it. We'll welcome constructive criticism, viewing it not as an attack but as an opportunity for growth.

We'll examine personal growth, recognizing it as an integral part of our identity formation. We'll embrace our imperfections and accept ourselves wholly, acknowledging that our flaws are as much a part of our identity as our strengths. And finally, we'll learn to push beyond our comfort zones, discovering facets of our identity that lie dormant, awaiting exploration.

By the end of this chapter, you'll have a clearer understanding of your unique identity and the tools necessary to nurture and celebrate it. It is my hope that you embark on this exploration with an open mind and an open heart, ready to embrace the beautiful individual you are destined to be. Let's dive into the journey of "Discovering My Identity."

What Are My Core Values and Beliefs?

Identifying our fundamental beliefs, or our core values, is akin to mapping the contours of our very identity. These guiding principles are the soul of our decision-making process, the architects of our worldview, and the framework of our personal and professional behaviors. They are the bedrock of our individuality.

To understand their importance is to understand the power of a compass in a vast ocean. Core values are our navigators in the tumultuous seas of life, providing direction amidst the waves of uncertainty and anchoring us when the storms of external influence bear down upon us. They lay the groundwork for our sense of self, highlight the areas of life that truly resonate with us, and help us channel our energies effectively. Moreover, these values become the mirror that reflects our actions, enabling us to introspect if our life is truly in harmony with our innermost beliefs.

Embarking on a journey to uncover your core values is an introspective endeavor. It begins with casting your gaze back upon the canvas of your life. Reflect on those instances when you felt a sense of deep satisfaction or a glow of pride. What actions led to those moments? Who were your companions on those journeys? What fundamental values were you upholding in those instances? The answers often shine a light on your core values. Conversely, reflecting on moments of dissatisfaction or frustration can also be enlightening, as such emotions frequently surface when our actions are at odds with our values.

The traits that you deeply admire in others also offer valuable insights into your own values. The virtues we respect in others often reflect our own cherished beliefs. Many self-help exercises and online tools are available as well, providing guided journeys into the realm of self-discovery.

However, the discovery of core values isn't a milestone to be achieved and left behind. As we make our way through life, evolving and growing, our values may shift and transform as well. Constantly revisiting and reassessing these values is a vital practice in personal growth, ensuring that we stay true to our authentic selves.

What Makes Me Unique and Why Is This Important?

Our uniqueness lies in the individual blend of characteristics, experiences, and personal history that sets us apart from everyone else. This uniqueness is especially important during our teenage years, a time when we are often tempted to blend in with the crowd due to social pressures and a desire to belong.

Being unique has its distinct advantages during adolescence. It fosters a sense of authenticity, an asset that aids in the development of a stable identity and paves the way for a strong sense of self-esteem. Uniqueness helps teenagers break free from the mold, encouraging them to make choices based on their values and interests rather than societal pressures. This cultivates decision-making skills, resilience, and self-confidence, all qualities essential for adulthood (Thoma & Dong, 2014).

Celebrating our uniqueness also has profound psychological benefits. It encourages self-acceptance and self-love, nurturing our mental health and well-being (Rodriguez et al., 2016). It equips us with a strong sense of purpose, direction, and fulfillment as our choices align with our true selves.

So, how can you identify what makes you unique? Start by exploring your interests and passions. What activities make you lose track of time? What topics do you enjoy learning about? Your interests often reveal unique facets of your personality. Also, consider your strengths and skills. What do others often compliment you for? What tasks do you find naturally easy? These are likely areas where you excel.

Reflecting on your experiences and personal history can also highlight your uniqueness. What life events have shaped you? How have these experiences influenced your perspective, values, and behavior? These reflections often unravel unique aspects of your identity.

Once you've discovered your unique traits, it's time to celebrate them. Embrace your quirks and eccentricities; they are the colors that paint your identity. Practice self-love and self-acceptance, and make choices that resonate with your true self. Be open and authentic about your uniqueness, as this promotes self-esteem and invites respect from others.

Finding and embracing your uniqueness is a journey of self-discovery and self-love. Remember, there's only one you in this vast universe, and that's your superpower.

How Can I Establish My Identity?

Navigating the teen years can feel like trying to find your way through a dense fog; everything seems uncertain and undefined. This section is all about pulling back that fog and revealing the path to self-discovery and personal identity.

Reflecting on your inner world, your thoughts, emotions, and experiences can act as your personal road map, illuminating the route to self-understanding. Make it a habit to turn inward, to take a good, hard look at what makes you tick, what matters most to you. This will serve as your guiding star on your journey to self-discovery.

Yet, looking within is just one piece of the puzzle. You also need to open your mind and heart to new experiences, cultures, and ways of thinking. This exposure to different perspectives can act like a light bulb, switching on to reveal aspects of yourself you never knew existed.

Even constructive criticism, while it may sting at first, can prove invaluable. It gives you a clear picture of how others perceive you and indicates where you might need to refine your behavior or approach. Take it in stride, learn from it, and use it to forge a more rounded and genuine sense of self.

Remember, forming your identity is a dynamic process; it evolves and grows as you do. Pursuing personal growth, be it acquiring new skills, overcoming challenges, or addressing personal weaknesses, helps you carve out an identity that's a true reflection of your potential.

Central to creating a personal identity is self-acceptance. This means acknowledging and embracing everything about yourself, your strengths, weaknesses, victories, and defeats. This acceptance allows you to construct an identity that is genuinely yours, not a carbon copy of societal expectations.

Finally, pushing your boundaries and venturing out of your comfort zone can significantly expedite your self-discovery. By tackling your own limitations and preconceptions, you can uncover your true potential and expand your sense of self.

As we look at each of these topics in more depth, I'll share relevant tips and practical advice. Keep in mind that finding your identity isn't a sprint; it's a personal, ongoing journey of exploration, understanding, and self-appreciation.

Practice Self-Reflection

Self-reflection stands as an indispensable pillar in the construction of your identity. It involves setting some time aside to dive deep into your mind, investigating your thoughts, feelings, experiences, and actions. This internal expedition enables a clearer understanding of your drives, decisions, and reactions (Rodriguez & Kelly, 2006).

Creating a steady routine of self-reflection can start with taking a few quiet moments each day to chronicle your inner world in a journal. This action can illuminate your attitudes, values, and behaviors while revealing recurring patterns or discrepancies. As you continue this practice, you'll gradually gain a deeper awareness of your life's shaping influences, the impulses that propel you, and the interests that set your spirit ablaze.

Another effective self-reflection method is meditation. Regular meditation practice can declutter your mind and bring your thoughts and feelings into sharp focus. It provides a safe haven where you can objectively observe your internal experiences, aiding a profound self-understanding (Lutz et al., 2008).

Indeed, self-reflection may lead you down some uncomfortable paths and force you to face truths you'd rather evade. However, these encounters with your less-pleasing sides are invaluable in your journey of self-discovery. This process isn't about tailoring a flawless image but about recognizing and accepting your true self in all its complexity.

Whether your chosen path is journaling, meditating, or perhaps a unique blend of methods, remember that regularity is crucial. Through continuous dedication, self-reflection can unlock the doors to a richer self-awareness, smoothing the road to identity development and promoting a more genuine and fulfilling existence.

Explore New Perspectives

Exploring new perspectives represents a crucial step toward establishing your unique identity. As we journey through life, we naturally accumulate a set of beliefs, biases, and assumptions based on our personal experiences and the influences around us. These views tend to shape our understanding of the world, dictating our responses and actions.

Venturing beyond your comfort zone to discover unfamiliar viewpoints helps broaden your horizon and deepens your understanding of yourself and others. By willingly stepping into the shoes of others, you can gain insights into their thought processes, emotions, and motivations. This exploration can lead to an improved understanding of human behavior and can significantly contribute to your personal growth and self-awareness.

Different ways to explore new perspectives include traveling, reading, participating in cultural exchanges, and engaging in open conversations with people who hold different viewpoints. Whether it's a book that challenges your worldview or a conversation with someone from a contrasting cultural background, each experience adds a piece to the puzzle of your identity.

For instance, travel provides an opportunity to immerse yourself in a new culture, offering firsthand experiences of different ways of life. It can help you question your ingrained beliefs and widen your understanding of the world. Similarly, reading can expose you to a wealth of ideas and perspectives, allowing you to explore the world through the eyes of others.

As you explore, keep an open mind and heart. Embrace the opportunity to learn and grow. Remember that every new perspective you encounter is an opportunity to refine your identity, adding color and depth to the picture you are painting of yourself.

Welcome Constructive Criticisms

Constructive criticism serves as a catalyst for our self-improvement. It invites us to view ourselves from a different perspective, highlighting areas where growth and enhancement are possible. Though it might initially seem tough to swallow, these feedback nuggets aren't meant to bring us down. Instead, they're shared to help us rise, pointing us toward areas where we could hone our skills or modify our behavior.

Consider this scenario, you submit an essay, and your teacher notes that you have a tendency to overgeneralize. Instead of viewing this as a personal attack, try to see it as guidance toward improving your writing skills. Taking their feedback on board, you focus on providing more specific and detailed arguments in your next essay. Not only does your writing improve, but you also demonstrate resilience and a readiness to learn from your errors.

Taking constructive criticism on board and utilizing it as a stepping stone toward self-improvement is a vital aspect of forming your identity. Each piece of advice you consider and apply nudges you closer to a more evolved version of yourself.

Seek Personal Growth

Pursuing personal growth is a lifelong process, an exploration of continuous learning and becoming better versions of ourselves. It's a self-driven journey filled with a desire to learn, expand personal consciousness, and realize the full extent of our abilities.

Everyone's journey to personal development is distinctly their own, shaped by individual goals, interests, experiences, and aspirations. This journey may involve learning a new language, acquiring a new skill, assuming a leadership role, or conquering a personal fear. It's the process of pushing your boundaries, accepting challenges, and drawing lessons from both successes and failures.

Let's consider the fear of public speaking as an example. By participating in a local debate club or signing up for a public speaking workshop, you're putting yourself in situations that challenge this fear head-on. Through regular practice and exposure, you gradually overcome this fear, growing not only in your ability to speak in public but also in your self-confidence and belief in your capabilities.

Emphasizing personal growth is an integral step in establishing your identity. As you evolve and grow, you gain a deeper understanding of your potential and aspirations. It's a journey where you are the explorer and the map, discovering more about your potential and, in the process, discovering more about who you truly are.

Embrace Imperfections and Self-Acceptance

Everyone has their own unique set of strengths, quirks, and, yes, even areas they may consider as shortcomings. Truly understanding ourselves means embracing this unique blend that makes us who we are, both the shining strengths and the areas we think need a bit of polish.

Here's the truth: nobody's perfect. We're all wonderfully human, and that comes with plenty of room for growth and development. Instead of letting these perceived imperfections drag us down, we should see them as opportunities for learning and self-improvement.

Self-acceptance isn't about making excuses for our mistakes or flaws. Rather, it's about treating ourselves with kindness and understanding when we stumble. It's acknowledging that we are valuable, just as we are, regardless of any imperfections we think we might have.

Imagine a person who believes they are overly sensitive, viewing it as a flaw. If they take a closer look, they might find that this sensitivity also makes them exceptionally understanding and empathetic toward others. In this way, what was once considered a flaw can be seen as a strength that forms an important part of their identity.

When we accept ourselves, warts and all, we open the door to personal growth. Once we acknowledge our flaws without judgment, we clear the path for positive change. It's only after fully accepting ourselves that we can see our potential for growth more clearly.

Pushing Beyond Your Comfort Zone

In the journey of self-discovery, one crucial step is to learn how to push beyond your comfort zone. This is the mental, emotional, and sometimes physical space where we feel safe and at ease. It's familiar, predictable, and, well, comfortable. But if we only ever stay in this zone, we limit our growth and hinder the development of our identity.

Exploring new experiences and taking risks is a fundamental part of understanding who we are and who we can become. When we dare to step out of our comfort zone, we expose ourselves to new ideas, challenges, and opportunities that can help us grow and evolve.

Think of a bird learning to fly. The nest is safe and comfortable, but staying there forever is not an option. The bird has to leap out of the nest, risking the fall, to ultimately soar in the sky. Just like the bird, we, too, need to venture out of our safe spaces to realize our full potential.

Pushing beyond your comfort zone might involve trying a new hobby, standing up for yourself, traveling to a new place, or even making new friends. It's about embracing the unfamiliar and the uncertain, knowing that it's okay to feel a little scared or uncomfortable. Because in that discomfort, we find growth.

But remember, pushing beyond your comfort zone doesn't mean dismissing your boundaries and doing things that compromise your safety or well-being. It's about healthy exploration, taking calculated risks, and continuously learning about ourselves. With every step outside your comfort zone, you're expanding it and making room for more growth, self-discovery, and resilience.

Remember that the journey of discovering your identity is unique to you. It's okay to take your time and navigate at your own pace. After all, self-discovery isn't a race but a lifelong journey filled with moments of realization, growth, and acceptance. Stay open, stay curious, and keep exploring the vast landscape of you.

Exercise: Identity Mapping Exercise

Materials: A piece of paper, writing materials, and colors (optional).

Draw a circle in the center of your paper, and write your name in it.

Next, surrounding your central circle, you can sketch additional circles that mirror the diverse components of your identity. This might encompass the roles you play in your life, such as being a student, a sibling, or a volunteer. You could also showcase your interests; maybe you're passionate about music, sports, or literature. Don't forget to highlight your personal values, integrity or empathy perhaps, and your strengths like creativity or perseverance. You might also want to include memorable life experiences that significantly impacted you and helped mold who you are today.

In each circle, write a brief description of what that aspect means to you. For example, under "music," you might write, "I love playing the guitar and writing my own songs."

For each aspect, think about its importance in your life. Is it a dominant part of your identity, or is it more peripheral? You can represent this by the size of the circles, bigger circles for more significant aspects, and smaller circles for less significant ones.

Now, think about how these different aspects connect with each other. Draw lines between circles that you feel are related. For example, you might draw a line between "volunteer" and "kindness" if you feel your volunteering experiences have cultivated your value of kindness.

Finally, step back and look at your identity map. Reflect on the following questions:

- What does this map tell you about yourself?
- Are there aspects of your identity that you'd like to explore or develop further?
- Are there new things you've discovered about yourself through this exercise?

Remember, your identity map is a snapshot of you at this moment. As you continue to grow and evolve, your map will change too. Feel free to revisit this exercise as many times as you want in your journey of self-discovery.

Chapter 3:

Finding Purpose and Meaning

The purpose of life is to live it, to taste experience to the utmost, to reach out eagerly and without fear for newer and richer experience. —Eleanor Roosevelt

I remember an intriguing story from when I was in high school that resonates with our topic at hand. My friend James, a self-confessed car enthusiast, used to spend hours tinkering with car engines or pouring over the latest car magazines. Although he wasn't exactly the class valedictorian, when it came to cars, he was like an encyclopedia on wheels.

We all thought it was just a hobby and that one day, he would outgrow it. But James saw something else. He saw a future intertwined with his love for automobiles. Today, he is an accomplished automotive engineer, much respected in his field. This story of James remains etched in my mind as a perfect illustration of how our passions can be the compass guiding us to our purpose.

Like James, you, too, have unique strengths, interests, and passions that can lead you to your purpose in life. In this chapter, we'll journey together to discover these elements, helping you identify what genuinely resonates with you. We'll explore what ignites your enthusiasm, what future you dream of, and the change you wish to see in the world. Our goal is to help you figure out your purpose and ultimately infuse your life with a profound sense of meaning and fulfillment. Let's get started!

What Are My Strengths and Areas of Improvement?

Discovering your unique abilities and the things you want to get better at is like finding hidden treasure in the big adventure that is your teenage years. This phase is all about changes, personal growth, and paving your own path, and knowing what you're really good at can help light the way toward finding what matters to you.

First things first: let's chat about your strengths. This could be anything that you're naturally talented at or simply love doing. Maybe you're a whiz at playing the piano, or you've got a knack for figuring out math problems. Or perhaps you're the friend everyone comes to when they need a listening ear or some kind words. The cool thing about identifying your strengths is that they're often linked to what you're passionate about, which can give you some clues about your purpose. By using your strengths as a compass, you can navigate toward a future that feels meaningful and authentic to you.

So, how can you figure out what your strengths are? A good starting point is to think about what activities you're drawn to or when you're doing something and lose track of time. Ask yourself, "What am I doing when I feel most proud or fulfilled?" It could be anything from taking the lead on a school project, creating a piece of art, or solving a tough riddle. Don't be shy to ask for opinions from people who know you well; they might have noticed things that you haven't spotted in yourself yet.

Knowing your areas for improvement is just as important. These are the parts of you that you could work on a bit more. It's not about focusing on the negatives but seeing them as chances to learn and grow. For example, you might absolutely love public speaking but get the jitters in front of a crowd. This is something you could improve, which would let you enjoy your passion even more and get you closer to your purpose.

Role models can be pretty handy when you're trying to figure all this out. Think about people who inspire you—what makes them stand out? What challenges have they faced and conquered? By looking at their journey, you might find qualities you'd love to see in yourself, or it could give you an idea of what path you might want to take.

By digging into your strengths and areas for improvement, you're giving yourself a chance to see where your abilities and passions overlap and where you can still grow. This self-discovery can guide you on your journey to finding your purpose and creating a life that truly feels like your own.

What Are My Interests?

You know that thrilling feeling when you're deep into something you love? That thing that lights up your eyes and makes your heart beat a little faster? That, my friend, is the magic of your interests at play. It's like unwrapping a gift that reveals a myriad of possibilities, and guess what? These interests often lead us on a fascinating trail to our purpose.

So, I want you to think about your interests. What are those things that fill you with enthusiasm and curiosity? It could be anything, an engrossing book that keeps you up all night, a hobby that lets hours slip by unnoticed, or even a burning question about the universe that you're itching to find the answer to. The key is to find what gives you a natural buzz, those activities that get your creative juices flowing and your spirits soaring.

Remember, though, there's a world of difference between passing fancies and true interests. Sure, the latest video game craze or the newest fashion trend can be fun, but I want you to delve deeper. Look for those interests that you believe will continue to spark joy and fascination even after the newness wears off.

One of the coolest parts about your interests is that they can help you make the most of your strengths. Picture this: You're an ace at problem-solving, and you're fascinated by environmental issues. This could point you toward a meaningful future in fields like environmental engineering or sustainability. You'd use your knack for solving problems to help protect our beautiful planet. How awesome is that?

This is another area where role models can help. They can inspire us with their stories of how they used their interests to create a life of purpose. Think about the people you admire, their interests, and their journey. Did their teenage passions play a role in shaping their life? How did they take those interests and turn them into something that made a difference? Learning from them can give you some serious motivation and a few handy tips to boot.

What Are My Passions?

Unleashing your passions feels a bit like lighting a match inside your heart. You just can't help but glow from the inside out, brimming with joy and vitality that's hard to hide. Your passion goes beyond a simple interest; it's a magnetic force that pulls you in, fueling your life with a profound sense of purpose.

Let's take a minute to think about what lights that spark in you. What activities get your heart racing? What dreams and ideas keep you buzzing with anticipation? Maybe it's an issue you feel strongly about, a hobby you adore, or a lifelong dream. These are your passions, the things that move you, make you feel alive, and ultimately infuse your life with real purpose.

Here's the great part about passions, they have a magical way of amplifying your strengths. For example, say you have a knack for leadership and are passionate about promoting mental health. You could harness your leadership prowess to spearhead mental health campaigns or organize events, thereby marrying your strengths with your passions. The outcome? A deep sense of personal satisfaction and a positive ripple effect in the world around you.

Again, consider the people you look up to, your role models. Reflect on how they've channeled their passions into purposeful paths. Learn from their determination, their journey, and the way they've made a difference through their passion. Their stories can become your roadmap, helping you chart your own course.

When you discover and nurture your passions, you're planting seeds for a life steeped in purpose. Your passions act like a compass, guiding you toward meaningful experiences, opportunities, and like-minded people. So, as you move on this exciting journey of self-discovery, always remember that your passions are your guiding stars, illuminating your path toward a rich and fulfilling life.

What Is Important to Me?

Understanding what matters most to you is like having a compass in the journey of life. It's especially true during your teenage years when you're starting to carve your own path. This compass, your core values and principles, the people you cherish, and the causes you believe in, is what helps you make decisions that align with your heart.

Imagine this: You're a natural when it comes to public speaking, and you deeply care about social justice. Combining these two, you could use your gift of gab to champion equality. This is how knowing what's important to you and linking it with your strengths can bring more meaning to your life.

If you're wondering how to start this journey of discovery, think about moments that made you feel genuinely happy and content. What were you doing then? Who was with you? Reflecting on these moments could give you clues about what really matters to you.

As you grow, it's natural that your priorities will change. So, remember to regularly take a step back and reassess what's important to you. This way, you'll ensure that you're always on a path that resonates with your heart, helping you live a fulfilling and meaningful life.

What or Who Inspires Me?

Inspiration can be a powerful guide, especially in our formative teenage years when we are trying to navigate our way to a meaningful life. The individuals or ideas that inspire us often shed light on the path we aspire to tread, offering a beacon to guide our actions and decisions.

Think about it this way, if you find yourself deeply moved by the story of a successful entrepreneur, for instance, it might reveal your latent interest in the field of entrepreneurship. It's not just about the achievements of this person that inspires you, but perhaps, the determination, creativity, and resilience they demonstrated in their journey, qualities you appreciate and would like to emulate.

You can further delve into this by asking yourself, "What particular aspect of their journey resonates with me? What did they do that I would also like to do?" These questions can help you better understand your inspirations and how they align with your innate strengths and interests.

In addition, inspiration doesn't have to be limited to individuals. It can stem from concepts, movements, or experiences that stir something deep within you. Whether it's the calm serenity of nature or the invigorating rush of a bustling city, the key is to identify what fuels your spirit and harness this energy to cultivate a sense of purpose and direction in your life.

Remember, these inspirations can also evolve as you grow, gain new experiences, and broaden your horizons. So, make sure to keep your mind open to new sources of inspiration that can guide you in your journey toward finding meaning and purpose.

What Kind of Future Do I Envision For Myself?

Let's get real for a moment. When you imagine your future, what does it look like? Don't worry about what seems practical or what others might think. This is your personal vision. Is it a certain job that piques your interest? Maybe a place you're yearning to live in or particular people you'd like to surround yourself with?

Your current circumstances shouldn't dictate what you dream about. Let's say you want to become a bestselling author, but you're currently grappling with your English homework. That's not a problem! After all, skills can be honed and enhanced. The crux is to figure out what sets your soul alight.

This exercise of visualizing your future serves two purposes. One, it shines a light on what excites you. Two, it helps you identify what skills or knowledge you need to work on to turn that vision into reality. So if you see yourself as an entrepreneur, it could be a good idea to delve into business studies or even kick-start a small project on your own.

Remember, the aim here isn't to put you on a rigid path. Instead, it's about providing a beacon to guide your steps. And if your dreams evolve, that's perfectly fine! The path you carve should be dynamic, changing as you grow and learn more about yourself.

This journey is not just about reaching the end goal; it's about the experience of getting there. It's about identifying your passions, pursuing them, and shaping a life infused with purpose. Don't hold back on dreaming big; start with small steps, and let your vision be your guide to personal growth and fulfillment.

What Kind of Change Do I Want to See in the World?

Close your eyes and think about your ideal world. What's different from how you see it today? Maybe you see more green spaces, equal opportunities for everyone, or new technologies making life easier. Whatever the vision, it's something that lights a fire in you, something you'd like to see change.

Now think about your role in that change. If you're excited about nature conservation, you might find yourself leaning toward a degree in environmental sciences or starting a neighborhood recycling program. Perhaps social equality strikes a chord, leading you to volunteer at a local shelter or pursue a career in social work. There's no limit to what you can contribute, and no contribution is too small.

Don't feel overwhelmed by the enormity of the world's problems; you're not alone in this, and every bit of effort counts. Your focus should be on what moves you, what aligns with your values, not what others might expect from you.

It's worth noting that your perspective might change over time. As you grow and evolve, so will your vision for the world, and that's a beautiful thing. The key is to stay true to yourself, aiming to make a difference in ways that feel genuine to you. After all, this journey is about finding purpose and meaning that resonate with your unique self.

How Can I Make a Positive Impact?

In the face of the world's challenges, it's easy to feel small and insignificant. But remember, everyone, no matter their age, has the potential to make a positive impact.

One of the most effective ways to make a difference is by leveraging your strengths. Maybe you're a natural problem-solver or a master at inspiring others with your words. These unique abilities can be utilized to promote change in your community and beyond.

Start small with actions that align with your values and passions. Volunteering at a local charity, starting a recycling initiative at your school, or even simply lending an ear to a friend in need, these seemingly small actions can have a big impact over time.

Remember, the goal isn't to solve all the world's problems in one swoop but to contribute to the change you wish to see in ways that feel meaningful to you. As you navigate this journey, remember that even the smallest ripple can lead to significant waves of change.

The journey of finding your purpose and making a positive impact might be challenging, but it's also rewarding. It offers a sense of fulfillment that comes from knowing you're contributing to something bigger than yourself. Stay true to your beliefs, embrace your strengths, and don't be afraid to step out of your comfort zone. Every step you take, no matter how small, is a step toward a more meaningful and purposeful life.

Exercise: Self Reflection

Time to put those thinking caps on for an exercise that will help consolidate all that we've discussed in this chapter. This exercise is all about self-reflection and brainstorming. You're going to dive deep into the essence of who you are and where you want to go in life. Grab a journal or a piece of paper and jot down your thoughts in response to the following prompts:

Explore your strengths: Write down what you believe your strengths are. These can be anything from being a great listener to having a knack for problem-solving. What skills or talents do you possess that make you feel confident?

Identify areas for improvement: Now, let's look at the other side of the coin. What areas would you like to improve? Remember, this isn't about criticizing yourself; it's about identifying areas for growth and self-development.

Interests: Let's make it a bit lighter. What are your hobbies? What activities do you find yourself drawn to in your free time? Write them down, and try to explore why you're interested in these areas.

Passions: Dig deeper into your interests now. Which activities make you lose track of time? What pursuits make your heart race with excitement? Identify your passions.

Remember, there are no right or wrong answers here. This exercise is just about you, a way for you to map out your strengths, weaknesses, interests, and passions. It's a journey of discovery that will help you carve out your path to finding purpose and meaning.

Take your time to thoughtfully answer each question. This is your chance to get to know yourself better, to reflect on what truly matters to you, and to begin painting the picture of the future you envision for yourself. Enjoy the process!

Chapter 4:

Making Meaningful Relationships to Boost Self-Esteem

We are born alone, we live alone, we die alone. Only through our love and friendship can we create the illusion for the moment that we are not alone. –Orson Welles

Picture this: you're at a party surrounded by people. You see groups of friends laughing together, people bonding over shared interests, and everyone seemingly having a good time. But despite the festive ambiance and the sea of friendly faces, you feel alone. Like you're on the outside looking in.

Growing up, I often found myself in this situation. I remember one instance clearly, a high school reunion where I felt like a fish out of water. Despite being surrounded by people I'd spent years with, I felt an uncanny sense of isolation. It was as if everyone had moved on and formed new alliances, and I was still stuck in the same place, unable to break the invisible barriers that held me back from making meaningful connections.

As I stood there, feeling like a wallflower, I had an epiphany; I was not alone in my loneliness. Many others were probably feeling the same way, grappling with the same sense of alienation. That's when I realized the value of interpersonal skills and building meaningful relationships. I started to learn, adapt, and grow, focusing not just on my relationship with others but also on the relationship I had with myself.

And so, in this chapter, we're going to explore the world of relationships, not just the ones we form with others but the ones we forge with ourselves. Together, we will navigate the challenging terrain of human connections, learning how to build, maintain, and value relationships that not only bring joy and companionship but also foster a healthy sense of self-worth.

What Obstacles Come in the Way of Relationships?

The journey of relationship-building is akin to traversing a landscape—ripe with exhilaration but also strewn with obstacles. We're venturing into a realm where challenges are but signposts, signaling a chance for learning and growth.

In this section, we'll discuss the roadblocks that are commonly encountered in the quest for forging strong relationships: dwindling confidence, communication mishaps, the intricate web of social media, competitiveness that overshadows collaboration, and the undercurrents of manipulation.

A deficit in self-confidence can leave us doubting our own worth, shutting us out from the possibility of cultivating fulfilling relationships. Misunderstandings born out of ineffective communication can fan the flames of conflict. Social media, while connecting us virtually, can lead to distorted perspectives, fueling unhealthy comparisons. Aggressive competitiveness can foster an "every man for himself" mentality, undermining the spirit of mutual support. Manipulation, often hard to detect, can gradually erode the foundation of trust in a relationship.

In the next section, we will go deeper into each of these barriers, exploring their origins, the impact they have, and, most crucially, the strategies to surmount them. After all, the journey toward meaningful relationships is marked by continuous learning and resilience.

Low Confidence

Let's consider low self-confidence like a heavy backpack we're carrying around all day. It's tiring and it's holding us back from moving freely and enjoying our journey. When our confidence is down, we might find ourselves second-guessing every move or avoiding social interactions entirely. It can make us feel like we're trapped inside a shell, just observing life from the sidelines but never fully participating.

There could be a million reasons why our self-confidence took a hit. Maybe a past situation didn't go as planned, or perhaps we've been on the receiving end of harsh words that still sting. These instances, unfortunately, can cause us to believe we're not worthy of positive and meaningful relationships.

Here's a crucial truth, though: Those old experiences, the cutting remarks, or that fear of getting rejected don't get to define who we are. Our worth isn't up for negotiation, and it certainly isn't decided by others.

Embracing self-confidence is less about putting on a flawless front and more about acknowledging and loving our true selves, flaws, quirks, and all. It's about realizing that it's perfectly okay to be a beautiful, evolving masterpiece. It's understanding that we are deserving of love, respect, and all the wonderful connections life has to offer.

Stepping onto the path of self-confidence might feel like a big leap, but remember, every journey begins with a single step. Every moment we spend nurturing our self-belief is a moment spent opening up to a world of more satisfying and meaningful relationships.

Poor Communication

Consider communication as a bridge that connects us to others. When it's solid and well-constructed, we can easily traverse back and forth, understanding and being understood, feeling valued and appreciated. However, when our communication skills are a little shaky, that bridge can become unstable, leading to misunderstandings, conflicts, and distance in our relationships.

So, what makes up "poor communication"? It might be not expressing ourselves clearly, or it could be that we don't listen well to what others are saying. Maybe we sometimes allow our emotions to overrun our words, leading to heated exchanges rather than open dialogue. Or perhaps, we hold back from saying what we really feel for fear of how others may react.

The consequences of this can be substantial. Misunderstandings can lead to hurt feelings, arguments, and a sense of disconnect. In turn, this can affect our self-esteem, making us feel isolated or underappreciated.

But here's the hopeful part, communication, like any other skill, can be improved. It starts with being honest with ourselves about where we might be going wrong. From there, we can learn to express ourselves more clearly, listen with empathy, manage our emotions in challenging conversations, and courageously say what we truly feel. In doing so, we build stronger, more meaningful connections with those around us, which in turn boosts our self-esteem.

Navigating the bridge of communication might feel daunting, but remember, every step we take toward better communication brings us closer to stronger, more fulfilling relationships. And with each successful crossing, our self-esteem grows.

Social Media

Imagine walking into a room filled with friends, family, acquaintances, and a few strangers, too, each one sharing glimpses of their lives, the victories, the vacations, the beautifully plated food. It seems like everyone has it all figured out. This, in essence, is what social media can often feel like, a constant stream of curated highlights, leaving us in a whirl of comparison and self-doubt.

Now, don't get me wrong. Social media isn't the bad guy here. It's a fantastic tool that connects us to people across the globe, allowing us to share our lives and experiences with others. But just like any tool, the impact it has on us depends on how we use it.

A significant challenge with social media is the tendency to compare our lives with others. We might find ourselves measuring our own worth based on the number of likes, shares, or followers we have, which can have a damaging effect on our self-esteem. It's easy to feel like we're falling short when we're constantly bombarded with carefully selected and filtered snapshots of other people's lives.

But here's the thing, social media is often a highlight reel, not an accurate depiction of someone's day-to-day life. So, when we compare our behind-the-scenes with someone else's highlight reel, it's not a fair comparison.

Building healthy relationships in the age of social media means understanding this fundamental reality. It also means learning to use these platforms in a way that uplifts rather than undermines us. This could involve curating our social media feed to include more positive and uplifting content, limiting our time on these platforms, and reminding ourselves that what we see online is not the whole story.

We can also use social media to foster meaningful connections by sharing more authentically, responding thoughtfully to others, and using these platforms to facilitate real-life interactions. In doing so, we can make social media a tool that supports rather than hinders our relationships and self-esteem.

Competition

Competition. We've all felt its presence in our lives. It's in the classroom, where we compare our grades with our classmates, on the sports field, where we strive to be the best player, and even in our social circles, where it sometimes feels like there's an unspoken contest of who's leading the most exciting life.

There's nothing inherently wrong with competition. In fact, it can be a powerful motivator, pushing us to improve, to grow, to strive for excellence. The thrill of the game, the satisfaction of a well-earned victory, there's a joy to be found in these moments.

However, when competition starts to seep into our relationships, it can turn corrosive. Friendships become a contest of one-upmanship. Family gatherings turn into a showcase of achievements. Every interaction is weighed and measured against a scale of success. We're no longer connected with people; instead, we're competing with them.

Competing with others can cause us to lose sight of our unique paths. We become so focused on outperforming others that we forget to question whether the race we're running is even one we want to win. This can be damaging to our self-esteem as we are constantly judging ourselves against others, often coming up short in our own eyes.

So how do we handle competition in our relationships? The key is to recognize it for what it is, a distraction. Yes, it's natural to want to compare ourselves to others. But it's more important to remember that we each have our own unique journey, complete with its own set of challenges, triumphs, and pace.

Instead of getting caught up in comparison, let's focus on our own growth. Let's celebrate our victories, learn from our defeats, and, most importantly, let's stop using others as our yardstick. When we focus on being the best version of ourselves rather than being better than someone else, we cultivate healthier relationships, foster positive self-esteem, and bring authenticity back into our lives.

Manipulation

Alright, let's talk about something a little tough: manipulation. It's that invisible puppeteer who tries to control your actions and thoughts, hiding in the shadows or dressing up as something more palatable. Believe it or not, manipulation finds its way into our relationships more often than we'd prefer to think.

Being manipulated feels a lot like being lost in a thick fog. It's disorienting, it's confusing, and it's scary. That's exactly what the person on the other end wants: they're aiming to tip the scales of power in their favor.

Here's the thing: a relationship that breeds manipulation is far from healthy. It undermines trust, steps over boundaries, and slowly but surely chips away at your self-esteem. If you're consistently the victim of manipulation, your self-confidence can take a hit. You may start feeling as if you're always in the wrong or never quite up to the mark. This can make you an easier target for more manipulation; it's a nasty cycle.

So, how can we tackle manipulation in our relationships? First and foremost, learn to spot it. Get familiar with the signs of manipulative behavior, making you feel guilty for no reason, gaslighting, or sowing seeds of self-doubt. If someone persistently leaves you feeling confused, guilty, or inadequate, it's time to pay attention.

Secondly, stand your ground. Draw the line where you need to. It can be tough, especially when the person pulling the strings is someone you're close to, but it's vital for your peace of mind. Remember, it's perfectly okay to say "no" and prioritize your own needs.

Lastly, don't hesitate to seek support. Open up to trusted friends, family, or a mental health professional. They can offer a fresh perspective, practical advice, and the emotional backup you need to navigate this tricky situation.

Handling manipulation is hard, no doubt, but it's a crucial step toward cultivating healthy relationships and fostering self-esteem. You are deserving of respect, honesty, and kindness, don't settle for anything less.

What Interpersonal Skills Do I Need?

Let's turn the page and look at the essential tools required for creating lasting, meaningful bonds. We're about to unravel the mystery behind interpersonal skills.

First off, let's talk about communication skills. It's quite like the magical key that unlocks any door of misunderstanding or miscommunication. Conveying our thoughts and feelings effectively and genuinely listening and understanding others is the foundation of any relationship.

Next, we wade into the unchartered territory of depth. Our lives are often a whirlwind of small talk and fleeting encounters. But forging deeper connections demands more; it asks us to be fearless and dive beneath the surface. Remember, the essence of any relationship lies not in the superficial but in the substantive.

After depth, we navigate our way to empathy. Picture it like walking a mile in another's shoes; you experience their reality, their joys, and their challenges. Empathy is a bridge that connects hearts and fosters stronger relationships.

Now we move to vulnerability and honesty. It may feel daunting to strip away the shields we're so accustomed to carrying to reveal our true selves, imperfections and all. However, vulnerability coupled with honesty paves the way for authenticity, making our bonds more profound and meaningful.

Then we reach the realm of conflict resolution. Disagreements, arguments, even fights, they're all par for the course in any relationship. But learning to navigate through these turbulent waters with grace and respect can mean the difference between a relationship sinking or sailing.

Lastly, we land on trust and confidence. Trust is the bedrock upon which relationships stand strong, and confidence is the flag we wave high, a flag that says, "I am capable, I am worthy." Together, they shape how we form and sustain relationships.

Communication Skills

When we think about forming and maintaining meaningful relationships, communication skills rise to the top of the list of essentials. These skills are more than just expressing our thoughts and feelings. They also include active listening, understanding, and responding appropriately.

Think about the last time you deeply connected with a friend. You didn't merely hear their words but also tuned into their body language, tone of voice, and underlying emotions. Active listening allows us to grasp the full essence of what's being shared and respond thoughtfully, making the other person feel heard and valued. That's how strong connections are built.

Moreover, expressing is more than just talking; it's about sharing ourselves honestly and openly, using our words, tone, and even silence in a way that is understanding and promotes connection.

But as with any skill, this one needs practice too. Improving our communication skills involves awareness, awareness of our own communication styles and habits and awareness of the other person's reactions and needs. As we grow in this awareness, we can adapt and refine our communication to better serve our relationships.

Let's pay attention to our communication, make every word count, and contribute positively to our interactions, enhancing our relationships and boosting our self-esteem in the process.

Depth

As we walk down the path of creating and nurturing meaningful relationships, we come across an essential factor, depth. Depth in a relationship is about the substance, the deeper connection that goes beyond superficialities. It's the glue that binds people together through the ups and downs, the calm and the storm.

Imagine depth as the roots of a tree. The bigger the tree, the deeper the roots need to be. Similarly, the more significant a relationship, the more depth it requires. But what does this depth consist of? Depth means building a shared history together, a range of experiences that enriches your relationship and strengthens your bond.

Yet, creating depth isn't always easy. To share ourselves deeply with someone else, we must first understand and accept our own selves, warts and all. It involves exploring our feelings and experiences, even the uncomfortable ones, and being willing to share them with others.

Furthermore, depth also means being receptive when others share their depths with us. When we respond with understanding, empathy, and respect, we create a safe space where the other person feels seen, heard, and valued.

In our quest for meaningful relationships, let's strive for depth. Let's be willing to dive beneath the surface and explore the beautiful, complex depths that every relationship holds. When we do, we find that deep connections feed our souls and enhance our self-esteem, making our lives all the more rich and fulfilling.

Empathy

Empathy is a word we hear often, but what does it really mean? And more importantly, why is it so crucial in our relationships?

Consider empathy as a pathway that binds us to others. Having empathy means possessing the capability to resonate with and comprehend the emotions of another, to figuratively walk in their shoes and witness the world from their perspective. It embodies the sentiment of being able to express, "I am here for all of you, the good, the bad, and the ugly."

But empathy is not just about understanding others; it's about demonstrating that understanding. It's about our actions, a comforting word, a supportive gesture, or just a listening ear. It's about making the other person feel seen, heard, and valued.

Empathy doesn't come naturally to everyone, but it is a skill that we can develop. By practicing active listening, being patient, and showing genuine interest in others, we can enhance our ability to empathize.

Remember, empathy is not about agreeing with others or sharing their exact emotions. It's about understanding their perspective, respecting their feelings, and responding with kindness and compassion.

Vulnerability and Honesty

Vulnerability and honesty are two words that carry so much weight in our lives and relationships, yet they're often the hardest to practice. They involve a certain amount of courage and a willingness to step into the unknown. But why are these qualities so important? Let's look deeper.

When we talk about vulnerability, we're referring to the willingness to show our authentic selves, our fears, our insecurities, our dreams, and our emotions. It's about letting our guards down and opening ourselves up to the possibility of being hurt. It sounds terrifying, doesn't it? But there's a kind of beauty in this raw openness, a strength in this perceived weakness.

Being vulnerable allows us to form deeper, more meaningful connections with others. By allowing others to see who we truly are, we're inviting them to do the same. It's a mutual exchange of trust and authenticity that forms the foundation of strong relationships.

On the other hand, honesty is about having the confidence to speak the truth, your truth, and standing up for what we believe in. It's about being clear about our intentions and our feelings. It's about treating others with respect and expecting the same in return.

Honesty promotes trust and respect in our relationships. When we're honest, we're showing others that we value them and their time. We're showing them that they can rely on us and that our words carry weight. This is essential for any relationship to thrive.

In essence, vulnerability and honesty are not just about our relationships with others. They're also about our relationship with ourselves. Let's strive to be vulnerable, let's strive to be honest, and let's watch our relationships flourish.

Conflict Resolution

In navigating life's choppy waters, we're bound to collide with others in the process. No two people are alike, and with difference often comes conflict. Most think that conflict is a red flag, a warning sign. In fact, it's quite the opposite; it's a crossroad, a junction for growth, understanding, and, ultimately, a deeper connection.

Conflict resolution is the compass that helps us find the way. It's a skill that involves active listening, patience, and emotional intelligence. Pretend you're arguing with a friend. You're certain you're right, but they think the same. Instead of heightening the tension, try taking a step back and inviting your friend to share their viewpoint without interruption.

The goal here isn't to win an argument. It's to better understand all of the perspectives involved and how they are in play. It requires us to show empathy, to put ourselves in their shoes. It also requires us to be open to the possibility that we may be wrong.

Conflict resolution isn't about dodging disagreements or brushing issues under the carpet. It's about confronting the conflict, understanding it, and working through it together. And when we do, not only do we resolve the disagreement, but we also fortify the relationship, proving that it can weather even the toughest storms.

Trust

Navigating the labyrinth of life, we find ourselves leaning on trust as a guiding principle. Trust, in essence, is the cornerstone of all relationships. It's that unwritten pact, an invisible thread that binds us together, letting us know we're safe, accepted, and, most importantly, understood.

How do we build trust? Trust isn't manufactured overnight. It's not a switch that can be flipped on when needed. It's an entity that requires nourishment, time, and consistent effort. It flourishes in an environment of honesty, openness, and reliability.

Keep your word. Even if it's about something as simple as returning a borrowed pen, do it. This demonstrates that you're reliable. Be transparent. Honesty may be tough, but it's a proven trust-builder. Understand the value of secrets. If someone confides in you, honor their trust. These are small steps, but together, they establish a strong foundation of trust.

Remember, trust is delicate. Once broken, it's tough, if not impossible, to regain. So, let's tread carefully on the path of relationships, nurturing trust with every step we take.

Confidence

Ah, confidence. That elusive trait we all wish we had a bit more of. It's the voice in your head telling you, "Yes, you can!" while simultaneously being the assurance in your heart that whispers, "You're enough, just as you are."

Confidence isn't about strutting around like a peacock or becoming the loudest voice in the room. It isn't about being impervious to criticism or never feeling nervous. Rather, confidence is embracing the understanding that you're a work in progress and that's okay. It's about acknowledging your strengths and weaknesses yet choosing to love yourself regardless.

So, how do we foster confidence? It starts with self-acceptance. You can acknowledge your flaws without letting them define you. Recognize your strengths, and celebrate them, no matter how insignificant they may seem.

Next, understand that it's okay to fail. It's natural to stumble and fall. Embrace it. After all, every fall is a chance to rise stronger. Also, stop comparing. It's a recipe for disaster. Your journey is unique, and so are you.

Practice self-compassion. Be your own cheerleader, not your worst critic. Speak to yourself like you would to a best friend in need. Would you belittle them or make them feel worthless? Or would you uplift them, helping them see their own worth? Choose kindness, always.

Lastly, invest time in doing things you love. It might be reading a good book, dancing like no one's watching, or perhaps baking cookies on a rainy afternoon. When you're engaged in something you truly enjoy, your authentic self shines through, and that's where true confidence lies.

Why Are Connections Important?

Connections in our life are like the strings on a guitar, each one vibrating to create a beautiful harmony. But have you ever wondered what makes these connections so important?

First, we'll unpack maintaining healthy vulnerability. Sounds a bit like a paradox, right? But it's about exposing your true colors, your authentic self, to others. It's about letting folks see the real, unvarnished you. This is the magic ingredient that brings us closer to others and deepens our bonds.

Next, we're going to chat about family. And no, it's not all about those folks you share a DNA with. We're talking about the ones you choose to call your tribe. These are the folks who influence our life's outlook and shape who we become.

Moving on, we'll swing the spotlight over to friendships. You know, those buddies who stick around because they just "get" you?' The importance of these pals in our life is huge, often reaching beyond the ties of family. We'll figure out why these relationships are so essential on our journey of life.

And finally, we'll look at the importance of other relationships. Here, we're throwing a wide net to catch all those interactions with colleagues, mentors, and even the stranger who lends a hand when we need it. We're going to uncover how these relationships, big or small, fill our lives with richness and play a big part in our overall happiness and personal growth.

So, come with us as we explore how each of these connections, vulnerability, family, friends, and other relationships, add threads to the social fabric of our lives, creating a sense of identity and a place where we belong. Let's get to it!

Maintaining Healthy Vulnerability

You know how we've always been told to "stay strong," "don't be a softie," or "never let them see you sweat"? Well, let's shake things up a bit. Let's admit that it's perfectly fine to show our softer side, our vulnerabilities. Believe it or not, being vulnerable can actually be a sign of strength!

When we talk about healthy vulnerability, we're talking about being real. It's about allowing yourself to be seen in your raw, unpolished state, with all your feelings laid bare. It's like giving someone a backstage pass to your private world of emotions and thoughts.

Now, you might be wondering, why should we even bother? What's the big deal about showing vulnerability? Well, here's the kicker, vulnerability is the secret sauce that makes connections deeper, richer, and more authentic. It's the birthplace of empathy, and it can supercharge our relationships. When you let your guard down and allow your true self to be seen, you're not only acknowledging your own humanity but also making it easier for others to show theirs.

Think about your closest friendships. Aren't they the ones where you can laugh together, cry together, and share your deepest fears without worrying about being judged? Or think about a relationship where you're free to express your feelings without the fear of being labeled "too sensitive." That's what vulnerability brings to the table. It creates a safe space for emotions and makes bonds stronger.

Now, I won't sugarcoat it. Being vulnerable can feel like walking a tightrope. It does expose us to potential heartache, criticism, and rejection. But let's remember, being vulnerable also means being brave. Courage and vulnerability are two sides of the same coin. It's in those moments when we let ourselves be vulnerable that we also show our greatest courage.

But let's not forget the "healthy" part of healthy vulnerability. It's about being smart about when, where, and with whom we share our soft underbelly. Not all situations require us to open up, and not all people can be trusted with our vulnerabilities. It's important to know when to open the door and when to keep it firmly shut.

So, what's the takeaway? Healthy vulnerability is a balancing act. It's about knowing when to shield ourselves and when to let our defenses down. It's about having the courage to be true to who we are and to share that truth with others. This can not only deepen our relationships but also make us more comfortable in our own skin. Remember, being vulnerable isn't a flaw; it's a superpower. It's a way of saying, "Here I am, with all my quirks and imperfections. And guess what? I'm absolutely fine with it!"

Family

You know, families remind me a lot of a well-loved quilt. Just go with me on this one! Picture every member of your family as a different, colorful square of fabric. Each square is unique and quirky, with a story only it can tell. When stitched together, these mismatched pieces transform into a beautiful, comforting quilt. And that, my friend, is family for you.

Our families are undeniably cornerstones of our lives. It's like our own personal boot camp. It's where we stumble through our first steps, muddle through our first words, and celebrate our first triumphs. In essence, our families are our first teachers, buddies, and allies. They shape our perceptions, principles, and personalities.

Have you ever just stopped and thought about the role your family plays? From the minute we're brought into this world, our family acts as our rock. It's the place where we're embraced, appreciated, and loved unconditionally. There's no need for any facade or pretense, just the authentic you.

Families aren't just about the warm fuzzies. They also serve as our first encounter with the dynamics of human relationships. Remember the squabbles with your sibling over the last piece of cake? Or the heated discussions with your folks? These experiences teach us about compromise, dialogue, conflict management, and, most importantly, forgiveness. Families, in a nutshell, mirror the wider world.

The beauty of the concept of family is its versatility. There's no one-size-fits-all here. Nuclear, extended, blended, adoptive, chosen—families come in all forms, each unique and special in its own way.

Sure, family relationships can sometimes be a bit tricky or a tad complicated. There might be rifts, disagreements, and rocky times. But that's just a part of life, isn't it? It's about how we overcome these challenges and learn from these experiences that truly matter.

To note, what if you do find yourself stuck in a toxic family environment? You're not alone, and there's something you can do about it. Think of family as those who truly care for you and make you feel good, not just those related by blood. Surround yourself with friends or people in your community who make you laugh, listen when you need to talk, and stand by you when you need support. It's all about building your own tribe of folks who genuinely want to see you thrive. After all, family is what you make of it, and sometimes friends become the family you choose.

At the end of the day, it's the blend of different characters, strengths, weaknesses, adventures, and idiosyncrasies that make a family, well, a family. So, treasure your family, celebrate the differences, and tackle the challenges with grace and patience. Because when it's all said and done, it's the bonds of family that keep us anchored, shape our identities, and build us into the people we become.

Friendships

If there's one ingredient that adds some serious sparkle to the recipe of life, it's friendship. Imagine life without friends. It's like a pie without the filling, right? Absolutely unimaginable!

Friendships are like little magical pockets of joy sprinkled throughout our lives. Think about it, a good friend's mere presence can make a boring day bright, a tough time bearable, and a joyous occasion unforgettable. That's some serious wizardry!

It all begins quite innocuously—a shared joke, a common interest, or even a mutual dislike (who hasn't bonded over a common enemy, right?). And before you know it, you've found your people—your tribe, your squad, your confidants. That's the beauty of friendship. It's not bound by blood, yet it's as potent as any familial bond.

Friends are our mirrors and our sounding boards. They reflect our strengths, gently point out our flaws, and give us a safe space to be unabashedly ourselves. They laugh with us, cry with us, dream with us, and grow with us. They teach us empathy, loyalty, resilience, and, most significantly, the importance of a good sense of humor.

And here's the real kicker, friendships come in all shapes and sizes. Childhood pals who've seen you grow, work buddies who make office life bearable, college mates who've survived the rigors of education with you, or digital friends whom you've never met yet share a deep connection with. Each of these friendships adds different flavors to our lives.

As we navigate through life, our friendships evolve. Some grow stronger with time, some may fade away, and that's perfectly alright. It's like the seasons, each has its own charm and purpose, and when one passes, another one arrives. So, too, is the case with friendships.

And remember, true friendships aren't just about sunshine and rainbows. Real friends are there with you in the eye of the storm. They stand by you in your darkest times, lending their strength when you're weak, their courage when you're scared, and their wisdom when you're lost.

In the grand scheme of things, friendships are the bonds we choose, the relationships we foster out of sheer affection and love. Here's to friendships, the unsung heroes of our lives, the chosen bonds that hold us together. Keep them close, nurture them, and cherish them. After all, they make the journey of life all the more worthwhile.

Other Relationships

Family and friends often steal the limelight when we talk about relationships that shape us, don't they? But have you ever paused to consider the subtle influence of those connections that linger on the fringes of our lives?

You know what I mean. Let's mull over those work mates, for starters. They aren't just people we spend eight or nine hours a day with. In fact, they're the folks who see us battle deadlines, handle stress, and celebrate little victories day in and day out. The chats over coffee, the brainstorming sessions, the shared sighs at the end of a demanding day, all of these things help us grow, even when we don't realize it.

Then, there are the teachers and mentors we meet at different stages of life. They're not just a source of knowledge or guidance; they push us to reach deeper within ourselves, embrace the challenge, and keep learning. They instill in us a love for learning and the courage to push past boundaries.

Within our own local communities, bonds bloom in unexpected places. The cheerful greengrocer, the kindly next-door neighbor, the local librarian who knows your taste in books, these small interactions add texture to our lives, helping us feel part of a larger, supportive network.

And how about those serendipitous connections we make? A stimulating conversation with a stranger in a coffee shop, a shared smile with a fellow dog walker, or a heart-to-heart with a backpacker on a train, these chance encounters often broaden our horizons in ways we never anticipate.

Last but not least, let's give a nod to our furry friends. They don't converse with us in human language, but the companionship and unconditional love they offer teach us some of the most profound life lessons.

So, when we talk about "relationships," it's important to remember these unsung heroes too. While they may not be in the spotlight, they play a significant role in coloring our lives, stretching our understanding of the world, and helping us grow. As we navigate through life, let's take a moment to appreciate these connections. They add depth to our life's narrative, making our story richer and more nuanced.

Exercise: Connect the Dots

Let's play "connect the dots."

Think back to those childhood games of "connect the dots." We'd take our pencil and, one by one, trace a line from each numbered dot until an image sprang forth, full of life and detail. Let's revive this game but this time, the dots are the many relationships in our lives, and the image is the shape and breadth of our personal growth. Ready? Let's play.

Step 1—The who: Take a minute and jot down all the important people in your life. Yes, all. Family, pals, the work buddy you share your coffee break with, the yoga teacher who helps you destress, the neighbor whose dog always greets you with a wagging tail. Try not to edit yourself here; no relationship is too small or too distant.

Step 2—The how: Beside each name, note down how they've left their imprint on you. Maybe your brother's constant joking has helped you develop your wit, or your colleague's dedication has inspired your work ethic. Don't forget that friendly dog; pets often teach us valuable lessons in unconditional love and loyalty.

Step 3—The what: Now, think about the pearls of wisdom you've gathered from these relationships and the personal growth you've experienced. Perhaps your best friend's steadfast loyalty has taught you the value of sticking by someone's side, or that high school teacher fostered a lifelong love for literature.

Step 4—The yet-to-be: Lastly, pinpoint one or two things you'd like to work on or improve in each relationship. These could be unexplored territories, newfound skills, or even a slight tweak in your own behavior or attitude.

This fun exercise allows us to fully appreciate the network of relationships we have, how they shape our lives, and how they contribute to our ongoing evolution. Every relationship, no matter how remote, carries a nugget of wisdom and adds a brushstroke to our life's canvas.

Don't forget to revisit your game of "connect the dots" from time to time. You'll find new dots added, older ones evolving, each change reflecting the ebb and flow of your personal journey.

So, pencil ready? Let's get started!

Chapter 5:

Overcoming Common Challenges

Hey, you made it here! You've decided to level up to unlock the cheat codes that will help you in this epic game we call adolescence. Welcome to the "Overcoming Common Challenges" chapter, your power-up guide.

Every teenager faces challenges. Call them bosses at the end of each level if you like. They come in many forms, from the anxiety-inducing world of social media to the mind-maze of peer pressure. Some of you might be grappling with mental health issues or getting bullied at school or online. And let's not forget those risky behaviors and addictions; they're like the sneaky, hidden traps in the game. Oh, and the ever-present academic pressures? Like the time limits that make every level more intense.

But hey, guess what? Every game, no matter how tough, has its power-ups, hidden paths, and the ability to respawn. In this chapter, we're going to explore some of these strategies.

Counseling might sound like an NPC (non-playable character) from a boring side-quest, but trust me; it can help boost your health bar. Support from the community? Think of it as your guild or party, ready to help when things get tough. Self-care is that save point where you get to heal and recharge. Patience, it's your shield, protecting you while you strategize. Being honest with yourself? That's the map that shows you where you are and where you need to go. And last but not least, courage, your mighty sword, is there to defend you against every boss you face.

Remember, this chapter isn't just a walkthrough to make the game super easy. Where's the fun in that? It's more about giving you the tools you need to tackle every challenge and enjoy the adventure along the way. Ready to level up? Great, let's hit start!

What Are Common Challenges That Teenagers Like Me Face?

So, here you are, avatar ready, game controller in hand, standing at the edge of this labyrinth we call teenage life. You may be thinking, "What kind of challenges am I supposed to expect? What do these "bosses" even look like?"

Fair questions, my friend. This section is your first level walkthrough, a spotlight illuminating the shadowy corners of the teenager's realm, making the unknown just a little bit less intimidating.

We're going to unpack common adversaries like mental health issues, the invisible but ever-so-real monsters that lurk beneath the surface. We'll break down the barriers of peer pressure, those pushy in-game characters always trying to dictate your path. And bullying, a vile creature that's been a part of this game for too long—we'll discover ways to deal with it.

But that's not all. You're living in the digital era; the landscape of social media is an integral part of your journey. It can be a tool or a trap depending on how you navigate it. Risky behaviors and addictions? Those are the game glitches that lure you off track. And let's not forget about academic pressures, the countdown timer that can turn even the simplest task into a frantic race.

In this section, we're going to face these challenges head-on, understand what they're all about, and find the strategies to conquer them. It's all part of the game, but remember, you're the player, and you have the power to shape your journey. Let's do this!

Mental Health Issues

So, here's the level that no one wants to talk about but everyone needs to hear: Mental health issues. Think of it as that misty, shadowy realm in your gaming world that everyone's too scared to enter. It's shrouded in mystery, often misunderstood, but dealing with it is a critical part of your journey.

Let's clear up one thing: encountering a mental health issue does not mean your game is over. Not at all. It just means you've stumbled into a challenging level that requires different strategies. Just like a game glitch that disrupts your avatar, mental health problems can disrupt your well-being. Anxiety, depression, eating disorders, or obsessive-compulsive disorder might be part of this realm.

You know, it's okay to feel the heat, to feel confused or scared in this level. It's okay to admit that your armor is heavy and your health bar isn't full. That's what this level is about: recognizing that it's okay to seek help, to look for health packs, or to take a pause and regroup.

This level is not about battling alone. It's about summoning your team, talking to allies (trusted adults, friends, or professionals), and understanding that you don't have to face these challenges by yourself. In this section, we will walk through this foggy terrain together, shedding light on the strategies to make it through.

Remember, it's your game, and every level is just another step toward becoming a more resilient, stronger player. Let's take this one step at a time, okay?

Peer Pressure

Alright, level two, get ready for this; it's the notorious peer pressure. You've probably heard tales of it from older siblings, friends, and teachers. It's like that boss level in your game that keeps coming back over and over. But here's the kicker, this boss doesn't fight fair. It doesn't always come at you head-on but rather sneaks up, influencing your choices and making you question your actions and values.

Peer pressure is a sly old fox. It comes in many disguises: from friends urging you to try a puff of that cigarette because "everyone's doing it" to that sense of urgency to maintain the perfect social media image just because it seems like the "in" thing. It could also manifest in subtler ways, like feeling the need to keep up with the latest trends or to hide your true passions because they're not "cool" enough.

And just like any other boss level, it feels scary. The thing about this boss is you don't beat it by going head-to-head. You don't need the most lethal weapon or the toughest armor. What you need is the shield of self-confidence and the compass of your values.

Navigating this level is about knowing that your game is unique and that your paths and choices are yours alone. It's about recognizing the difference between healthy influence and forceful pressure. The trick is not in defeating this boss but in outsmarting it, making decisions that align with your values, not what the crowd pushes you toward.

Bullying

Okay, buckle up because we're about to tackle a biggie. This level isn't just difficult; it's personal, it's real, and sadly, it's all too common. We're going to address the elephant in the room, bullying. It's like that overpowered, unfair enemy in the game that nobody wants to face, but too many of us do in one way or another.

Bullying comes in many forms and wears many masks: hurtful words, social exclusion, gossip, online messages, or physical aggression. It's not just being shoved into a locker or having your lunch stolen. It's that snide comment about your weight, the rumors about your family, the group chat you're purposefully left out of, or the embarrassing picture circulated online. It's cruel, it's damaging, and it's far from the fair play we expect in the game of life.

Facing this level can feel like the whole world is against you, but remember, it's just a level, and it won't last forever. It may feel overwhelming, but like every difficult level in every game, it doesn't define you, and it doesn't define your worth.

Here's the thing, though, this level isn't one you should have to face alone. The way to overcome this challenge is by reaching out, assembling your squad, and rallying your support system. That means talking to friends, trusted adults, or even reaching out to counselors and hotlines when things get too tough. Because just as in any co-op game, teamwork makes the boss levels manageable, and in the game of life, it's no different.

Social Media

It's time to dive into a level that can seem like it's all bright lights, sparkle, and instant gratification, but hold up... let's take a pause and look a little closer. It's social media, the space where everything is supposed to be fun, connected, and exciting... until it's not.

You know what I'm talking about, right? That feeling of scrolling through posts that show perfect people living their perfect lives with their perfect friends and their perfect pets. It's like entering a world where everything is a glossy, perfectly-lit highlight reel. And while we know deep down that there's a ton of smoke and mirrors involved, it can still get to us. We start to compare our lives, our looks, our achievements with those shiny posts, and suddenly, we feel like we're not measuring up.

But let's get real, who among us can honestly say that what we post on social media is the complete, unfiltered truth of our lives? It's a curated version, the "best hits," if you will. No one is posting about their bad hair days, their low marks in Algebra, or the argument they had with their best friend.

So, the trick with social media is to remember it's like a game within a game. It can be a ton of fun and a great place to connect, but it isn't the whole story. Comparing your "behind-the-scenes" with someone else's "highlight reel" isn't just unfair; it's setting yourself up for a level of perfection that doesn't exist.

But here's the secret sauce to this level, it's all about balance and setting your own rules. Limit your time, be picky about who you follow, and remember to use social media as a tool for connection, not comparison.

Risky Behaviors and Addictions

Now, here's the thing about being a teenager, it's a stage full of questions, rebellion, and new discoveries. Picture it as a vast gaming arena, where we are the player-characters learning the ropes, figuring out the gameplay, and maneuvering through different levels. It's exhilarating and downright nerve-wracking. One such bumpy stretch is the level of risky behaviors and addictions. It's a tough topic to navigate, but absolutely necessary because it is a very tangible part of being a teenager.

As we level up in the game of life, the thrill of newfound independence can sometimes make us take on challenges that we may not be ready for; these are the "risky behaviors." Maybe it's sneaking out for that late-night party or caving into pressure to try smoking or drinking just because it seems like all your friends are doing it. Or, it could be the fast-beating thrill of making risky bets online or speeding up because it feels liberating.

But let's pause the game for a moment. Here's where we need to use our in-game strategy and decision-making skills. Remember, it's not about avoiding risks completely but about understanding the consequences and making informed decisions.

Then there's the big boss battle, addictions. Be it dependency on substances, an unhealthy attachment to the online world, or being an obsessive workaholic (yes, there's such a thing as gaming too much!), addictions can sneak up on us. They start as seemingly harmless habits that we're sure we have under control until one day, we realize we're the ones being controlled.

Navigating these treacherous levels is tough, but here's the good news, you're not alone. We're all in this multiplayer game together, helping each other spot the danger signs, understand the why behind them, and, most importantly, learn to avoid falling into these pitfalls.

Academic Pressures

Let's take a moment to acknowledge the giant, fire-breathing dragon in the room—the ultimate boss level of teenage life, better known as academic pressures. Just hearing that term is enough to cause a shiver down your spine, isn't it?

In this epic battle, your weapons are your textbooks, your potions are cups of caffeine, and your power-ups are the hard-earned grades you're aiming for. But despite your valiant efforts, it feels like the dragon keeps gaining HP, and you're running out of lives faster than you can say, "Game Over."

Academic pressures can come in all sorts of shapes and sizes, from pushing yourself to cram an entire semester's worth of knowledge in one night to stressing out about a test that could make or break your report card. And let's not forget the scary specter of college admissions hovering ominously in the background.

It can often feel like you're playing this boss level on hard mode, with every minor setback seeming like a major catastrophe. Your mind races, palms sweat, and suddenly it feels like you're facing a horde of monstrous, undefeatable tasks, each scarier than the last.

But remember, gamer, every level, no matter how challenging, has its weaknesses. It's all about strategizing, planning, and taking breaks when needed. Yes, even the toughest warriors need to retreat and regroup sometimes. And most importantly, don't forget to celebrate your wins, big or small. Every quest completed, every dragon slain, brings you closer to your ultimate goal.

How Do I Overcome Challenges in My Teenhood?

Having opened up the suitcase of common challenges that you, as a teenager, might face, from academic pressures to the unexpected trials of social media, it's time to look at what you can do to tackle these head-on, no matter how tough they may seem.

Overcoming challenges isn't about snapping fingers and making them disappear. Instead, it's about getting to grips with them, finding ways to navigate around or through them, and learning from them to build resilience and strength.

For this task, there's a toolbox at your disposal. Guidance or counseling can be that compass that gives you a sense of direction when things get confusing. Support from your community, your family, friends, or even trusted adults, is like the sturdy rope you can rely on when the terrain gets tricky.

Self-care is your necessary pit-stop, allowing you to replenish your energy and regain focus. Patience is the steady drumbeat that keeps you moving at your own pace, reminding you that no hurdle is insurmountable with time and persistence. Honesty with oneself is your headlamp, illuminating the areas you need to work on, while courage acts as the fuel that propels you to keep trying, even when things seem daunting.

By using these tools, you're not just going to weather the storms of your teenhood; you're going to learn to navigate through them, turning each challenge into a step on your journey of personal growth.

Guidance or Counseling

Let's chat about the idea of seeking guidance or counseling. Yeah, yeah, we know what you're thinking, "I'm not a kid anymore; I can handle my own stuff." Sure, you're older now and there's a certain kind of satisfaction that comes from figuring things out by yourself. However, picture this:

You're building a LEGO masterpiece; maybe it's a castle with a dragon or a skyscraper that kisses the clouds. Either way, it's a huge project. Now, you could do it all by yourself, spending hours, maybe even days, trying to find the right pieces and put them in the right places. But wouldn't it be so much easier, not to mention quicker, if you had the instruction manual handy?

Guidance or counseling is kind of like that instruction manual. They're resources that can provide a map of the sometimes-confusing city of adolescence. They can help illuminate the blind spots in your understanding and equip you with strategies to manage whatever is going on in your life.

Counselors or trusted guides don't exist to judge you, laugh at you, or scold you. They're there to listen, to understand, and to offer helpful advice or solutions. They're trained to deal with all kinds of issues, whether it's academic stress, relationship worries, or that nebulous feeling of not-quite-right that sometimes settles in your stomach.

Remember, asking for help doesn't make you weak or incapable; on the contrary, it's a sign of strength and maturity. By seeking guidance or counseling, you're taking an active step to take charge of your life and your feelings. So next time you're feeling stuck or overwhelmed, remember your LEGO instruction manual—no shame, no harm, only help.

Support and Community

Picture this: you're the star player in a basketball game. You've got the ball, and you're racing toward the hoop, the crowd is cheering, and it's exhilarating. But you're not alone on that court. There are four other players on your team, all backing you up, ready to take the pass, block the opposition, and help score that winning shot. They're your support, and without them, the game would be a whole lot tougher.

In much the same way, the game of life isn't meant to be played solo. Everyone needs a team, a community, to back them up. This could be family, friends, mentors, teachers, coaches, or even online communities of people who share your interests or challenges.

Your community provides the emotional support that can uplift you when you're feeling down, provide a listening ear when you need to vent, and offer a high-five (literal or virtual) when you've accomplished something you're proud of. They can also provide practical support, like helping with homework, teaching you new skills, or giving you advice based on their own experiences.

It's important to remember that being part of a community isn't just about receiving support; it's also about giving it. Supporting others can provide a sense of purpose and fulfillment and also helps strengthen the bonds within your community.

So, next time you're feeling overwhelmed, remember that it's okay to pass the ball. Reach out to your community, ask for help, and let them support you. Life's a team sport, after all.

Self-Care

Now, imagine you're a high-performance car. Yeah, like one of those slick, shiny sports cars that roar with power and purr with finesse. This car is your life, and you're both the driver and the mechanic.

Now, you wouldn't expect a high-performance car to keep running smoothly if it's not looked after, would you? It needs the right fuel, regular servicing, and a good clean now and then. Well, you, my friend, need the same. That's where self-care comes in.

Let's start with the basics: eating well, getting regular exercise, and making sure you're getting enough sleep. These are the essentials, your high-octane fuel, and without them, your engine will start to splutter.

But self-care goes beyond just the physical. It's also about taking care of your mind. This could mean a range of things, from taking some time each day to relax and do something you enjoy to practicing mindfulness or meditation to help manage stress.

There might be times when you think, "I don't have time for self-care; I've got too much going on." But remember, you can't pour from an empty cup. It's important to take the time to recharge so you have the energy to tackle everything else on your plate.

In other words, self-care isn't just about feeling good; it's about maintaining your engine so you can keep up with the fast-paced race that is teenage life. So, remember to take that pit stop once in a while; your body, mind, and life will thank you for it.

Patience

Let's get real for a moment. Being a teenager can feel like you're stuck in the world's longest queue. You're waiting for everything, waiting to graduate, waiting to get your driver's license, waiting to become an adult. It's like you're always on the edge of something big, and it just can't come fast enough. I get it; waiting can be tough, and having patience can feel like a chore. But guess what? It's also one of the most vital skills you can master during your teen years.

Patience, you see, is not just about twiddling your thumbs and staring at the clock. It's a form of action, a conscious choice to hold your ground and keep your cool even when things aren't going as fast as you'd like. It's about understanding that good things often take time, and the most worthwhile rewards aren't always immediate.

Now, I'm not saying it's easy. When that anxiety of waiting starts to creep in, it can feel like a swarm of ants marching up and down your body. But the more you exercise patience, the more you build resilience, a kind of mental and emotional muscle that makes you stronger in facing the world.

Remember that high-performance car we talked about? Even it doesn't go from zero to sixty in zero seconds flat. It takes time to accelerate. Much like life itself, the journey to your dreams and goals is not a race but a steady drive. So buckle up, hold the wheel steady, and remember: even a red light is temporary. Your green light is coming, and when it does, you'll be ready to move forward with grace and confidence.

Honesty With Oneself

Teenage years are a roller coaster, aren't they? It's like you're on this wild ride of self-discovery, figuring out who you are and what you stand for. And on this path, one of your most reliable guides can be honesty with oneself. It might not always show you what you want to see, but it will definitely show you what you need to see.

What do I mean by "honesty with oneself"? It's the courage to accept and understand your true feelings, thoughts, and actions without sugar coating or self-deception. It's about looking at yourself in the mirror, metaphorically speaking, and seeing who you really are, warts and all.

Think about when you're playing a video game. It's so easy to blame a loss on the game mechanics, a faulty controller, or even the pizza guy who interrupted you at a crucial moment. But the best gamers? They own up to their mistakes. They acknowledge where they could have done better and use that insight to improve.

In the same vein, being honest with yourself about your strengths, weaknesses, and everything in between allows you to grow in a way that nothing else can. You can't fix a problem if you don't admit it's there. You can't celebrate success if you don't admit you earned it.

Being honest with oneself doesn't mean you have to be hard on yourself. It's not about focusing on flaws or mistakes. It's about acknowledging them as part of who you are and understanding that they don't define you. Every stumble is a learning opportunity, and every achievement is a step forward on your journey.

The beauty of honesty with oneself is that it opens the door to genuine self-improvement and self-love. It's not always an easy door to open, but trust me, the room behind it is filled with potential. And the person you discover there—the real you—is definitely someone worth knowing.

Courage

Let's talk about courage. Now, I know what you're thinking, "Oh, courage is for superheroes in comic books or characters in action-packed video games." But that's where you'd be wrong. Courage isn't just for the superheroes we admire on screens; it's for you and me. It's for every teenager who dares to face the high-school drama, the looming academic pressures, the heartbreaks, and the triumphs.

So, what exactly is courage in the real world? It's not always about dramatic gestures, like rushing into a burning building to save a cat, although those instances are indeed courageous. Real-life courage can be much more subtle but no less significant. It's the guts to say "no" when everyone else is saying "yes." It's the determination to stand by your values, even when they're not popular. It's the boldness to express your thoughts and emotions authentically, even if you fear judgment or rejection.

And hey, remember when you faced that super tough level in your favorite video game? You were probably scared of losing, perhaps even tempted to switch off the console. But you didn't. You stuck with it, faced the challenge head-on, learned from your mistakes, and eventually triumphed. That, my friend, is courage in action.

As you journey through your teenage years, you'll encounter various challenges and pressures that may seem insurmountable. It's normal to feel scared, anxious, or even overwhelmed. But remember, it's okay to be scared. Courage isn't about being fearless; it's about acknowledging your fears and stepping forward anyway.

In fact, every bit of courage you demonstrate, no matter how small, helps you build resilience and self-confidence. It fuels your growth and empowers you to conquer the challenges that come your way. In essence, courage helps you unlock your potential and become your own superhero. So go ahead, put on your invisible cape, and embrace the power of courage. You've got this!

Exercise: Drawing Out Your Bravery

Now, it's time to transform our insights into action. Let's do an exercise that fosters self-discovery and builds up your bravery. Here's a three-part plan to get started:

Part 1: Spotting the scaries

Start by scribbling down a list of what's scaring you or stressing you out these days. Maybe it's a looming presentation in front of your classmates, speaking up for yourself or someone else, or a seemingly insurmountable school project.

Part 2: Bravery blueprint

For each thing that's freaking you out, brainstorm one specific action you can take to face that fear head-on. You might rehearse your presentation in front of your pet, role-play tricky conversations with a trusted friend, or break down that mega-project into mini-tasks. Remember, bravery isn't about being fearless; it's about moving forward even when you are scared.

Part 3: Looking back to move forward

Make a note to revisit your list in about a month's time. Reflect on the headway you've made. Have you faced your fears? How does it feel when you tackle things that used to scare you? Appreciate your progress and celebrate your triumphs, no matter how tiny they might seem. And if you feel like you're stuck in the same spot, don't beat yourself up. Bravery is a marathon, not a sprint.

This hands-on approach won't just help you face your fears; it will empower you to take the reins of your life. And don't forget; it's completely okay to lean on your support network as you embark on this adventure. You're not in this alone and every little stride you make is a win. So, harness your inner strength and let your bravery shine through.

Chapter 6:

Succeeding in School and Beyond

Welcome to the last chapter of the book "Succeeding in School and Beyond," where we'll explore strategies for succeeding in school and building a fulfilling life. This is going to be fun; we'll be tackling some big questions together, like "What motivates me?" and "How can I manage anxiety?"

We'll start with motivation. It's like rocket fuel for chasing your dreams. But where does it come from? How do we get more of it? We'll explore that. And yeah, anxiety sucks, but it's a normal part of being human. We'll talk about healthy ways to handle it so it doesn't get in your way.

We'll also chat about things like personality, handling stress, and beating procrastination. All the stuff that comes with being a student! If you ever feel lost or like you just can't get going, we've got you covered. And we'll figure out how to stop comparing yourself to other people; that's a game you can never win.

Here's the exciting part, we'll dig into who *you* want to be. What makes you leap out of bed in the morning? What are you passionate about? Let's uncover the real you.

We'll also get practical: how to set goals, manage time, and learn to say no when you need to. You know, work smarter, not harder type of skills. And we'll create habits to make studying less of a chore.

As we wrap up, we'll talk about perseverance and grit—keeping going even when life gets bumpy—because it will! But that's okay. Let's get started.

How Do I Find Fulfillment?

What does it mean to live a fulfilled life? That's the big question we'll be tackling in this section. Finding true fulfillment is tough; we all have those days when we feel bored, anxious, stressed to the max, or just feel lost. You're not alone! The good news is there are some simple mindset shifts and strategies that can help get you pointed toward a path of greater joy, purpose… and, yeah, fulfillment.

Together we'll chat about how to get motivated when you're feeling apathetic, deal with anxiety when it rears its head, and get to know yourself on a deeper level. Understanding your personality and what makes you tick is key! We'll also talk about managing stress when life gets overwhelming, avoiding unhealthy comparisons that leave you feeling crummy, and eliminating distractions that stand in the way of what matters most.

Here's the deal: Fulfillment looks different for everyone. What fires you up might leave me cold, and vice versa. But no matter our differences, there are some universal tools we can use to carve out a life that feels meaningful. I don't have all the answers, but I've picked up some insights over the years, and I'm excited to share them with you in the hopes they will help you advance your own journey. Sound good?

Find Motivation

A question often lurking in the back of our minds as we navigate the maze of education and early career choices is, "How do I find fulfillment?" The journey begins with one crucial step, finding motivation.

Motivation is the wind in your sails, propelling you forward in your academic voyage and your personal and professional growth. It's an intrinsic force that urges you to push boundaries, strive for excellence, and keep marching on, even when the path is steep and littered with obstacles.

So, how does one discover this magical catalyst known as motivation? It starts with a simple introspection. Delve into your core, explore your interests, identify your strengths, and acknowledge your weaknesses. What gets your heart racing? What fills you with a sense of accomplishment and satisfaction? The answers to these questions often point toward your true passions and aspirations. When you're driven by passion, motivation doesn't feel imposed or laborious; it springs naturally, brimming with enthusiasm and excitement.

Next, set academic and personal goals that align with your passions. These goals act as beacons, illuminating your path and providing a clear direction. They add purpose to your efforts and make the journey toward achievement more fulfilling.

Remember, motivation and fulfillment in school and beyond aren't solely tied to grades or conventional definitions of success. They're intricately connected to your personal growth, sense of accomplishment, and the joy you derive from learning and evolving. It's about finding contentment in your journey, celebrating small wins, learning from setbacks, and constantly evolving.

Finally, bear in mind that motivation isn't a constant. It ebbs and flows, just like the ocean tides. There will be periods of high motivation, where you feel invincible, and periods of low motivation, where everything seems challenging. In these low tides, don't be too hard on yourself. Seek support, embrace self-care, and remind yourself of your "why."

In essence, finding motivation, the cornerstone of fulfillment in school and beyond is a personal, ongoing journey. It's about aligning your actions with your passions, setting and pursuing meaningful goals, embracing the joy of learning, and remaining resilient through the highs and lows. It's your journey, and with the right motivation, you can certainly make it fulfilling.

Deal With Anxiety

When we tread on the path toward fulfillment, anxiety often emerges as a frequent, unwelcome companion. The pressures of academic performance, the expectations from family and peers, and the uncertainty of the future—all these factors can trigger waves of anxiety. Yet, dealing with anxiety effectively is an integral part of finding fulfillment in school and beyond.

First, it's crucial to acknowledge that experiencing anxiety is entirely human. It's a natural response to stress, and everyone experiences it in one form or another. Recognizing anxiety, rather than denying its existence, is the first step toward dealing with it.

Once you've identified your feelings of anxiety, self-compassion becomes your best ally. Often, we're our harshest critics. Replace that inner critic with a supportive friend. Remind yourself that it's okay to feel anxious and that it doesn't define your worth or potential.

Now, let's dive into some practical ways to deal with anxiety. Mindfulness is a powerful tool in this regard. It's all about anchoring yourself in the present moment, letting go of past regrets and future worries. Regular mindfulness exercises, such as deep breathing, meditation, or even a simple walk in nature, can alleviate anxiety and foster a sense of peace.

Another key element is maintaining a balanced lifestyle. Regular exercise, a nutritious diet, adequate sleep, and recreational activities are not just essential for your physical health, but they also contribute significantly to your mental well-being. Remember, a healthy mind resides in a healthy body.

Stay connected with your support network, friends, family, mentors, or counselors. They can provide a listening ear, comforting words, or practical advice when anxiety looms large. Remember, it's okay to ask for help.

Lastly, develop healthy coping mechanisms. This could be anything from reading a book, journaling your thoughts, practicing yoga, or indulging in a hobby. Find what works for you and incorporate it into your routine.

Dealing with anxiety is not about eliminating it completely; that's neither possible nor necessary. Instead, it's about managing it effectively so it doesn't hinder your path toward fulfillment. With the right mindset and tools, you can navigate through anxious moments and continue your journey toward succeeding in school and beyond, imbued with a newfound sense of resilience and calm.

Understand Your Personality

As we sail through the sea of education, success often seems like an objective benchmark, a standard set by scores, rankings, and traditional accomplishments. Yet, true fulfillment lies not in adhering to a one-size-fits-all path but in acknowledging and embracing your unique journey. To set sail on this journey, understanding your personality is the compass you need.

Your personality is a beautiful blend of your traits, values, beliefs, and behaviors. It's a mix of what makes you tick, what drives your passion, and how you interact with the world around you. Understanding your personality can empower you to align your educational pursuits and life choices with your natural inclinations and strengths, leading to a deep sense of fulfillment.

Start by exploring various personality frameworks, such as the Myers-Briggs Type Indicator (MBTI) or the Big Five personality traits. These are not definitive labels but insightful tools that can offer a deeper understanding of your key traits and tendencies.

Next, pay attention to your intrinsic motivations. What activities excite you? What tasks do you find energizing, and which ones drain you? These subtle cues often reveal significant insights about your personality.

Embrace introspection as your regular companion. Journaling, meditation, or simply spending quiet time alone can shed light on your thoughts, emotions, and responses, thereby providing clues about your personality.

Remember to celebrate your strengths but also accept your weaknesses. Nobody's perfect, and that's okay. Recognizing areas of improvement doesn't diminish your worth; it offers opportunities for growth and learning.

Understanding your personality also aids in fostering healthier relationships with your peers, teachers, and family. When you comprehend your communication style, emotional responses, and conflict resolution strategies, you can navigate social interactions more effectively.

Moreover, comprehending your personality can guide your career decisions, helping you choose paths that resonate with your core interests and work-style preferences. This alignment can lead to a more satisfying and fulfilling professional life.

In essence, understanding your personality is like getting acquainted with the most consistent companion in your life, yourself. As this self-awareness deepens, you'll be able to make choices that resonate with your true self, leading to a sense of fulfillment that is genuinely yours. This understanding becomes your guiding star, illuminating your unique path to success in school and beyond.

Manage Stress and Fatigue

It's no secret that the pursuit of academic success and personal growth can sometimes feel like running a marathon with no finish line in sight. Assignments pile up, exams loom ahead, social commitments call, and somewhere in the middle of all this, you're expected to plan your future too. No wonder stress and fatigue can sneak into our lives, casting a shadow over our motivation and joy. Yet, managing these silent invaders is key to finding true fulfillment during your educational journey and beyond.

Think of stress and fatigue as the red flags your mind and body wave when they need your attention. They are signals prompting you to slow down, reassess, and rebalance. Paying heed to these signals, acknowledging them, and taking proactive steps to address them, paves the way for a more balanced, fulfilling life.

Adopting stress management techniques like mindfulness, deep breathing exercises, and regular physical activity can provide immediate relief. Creating a quiet, mindful moment in your day to simply sit, breathe, and be present can work wonders in reducing stress levels. Engaging in regular physical activity, be it a brisk walk, yoga, or a quick dance-off with your favorite tunes, releases endorphins, your body's natural stress busters.

Next, ensure you're fueling your body with a balanced, nutritious diet. Foods rich in omega-3 fatty acids, like fish and walnuts, and vitamin C, like oranges and strawberries, can help combat stress. Staying well-hydrated is equally important.

Sleep, the underrated hero of stress management, deserves special mention. Cultivating a regular sleep routine, prioritizing quality sleep, and creating a sleep-friendly environment can dramatically improve your energy levels and stress resilience.

As for fatigue, it often stems from overcommitting and not allocating enough time for rest and recreation. Learn to recognize your limits and respect them. It's okay to say no to extra commitments when you're feeling stretched thin. Balance your work and study time with hobbies and activities that refresh and rejuvenate you.

Lastly, remember that seeking professional help is a sign of strength, not weakness. If stress and fatigue persist despite your best efforts, reaching out to a school counselor, a therapist, or a trusted adult is a brave and important step.

Learning to manage stress and fatigue is an ongoing journey, but it's one that leads to resilience, well-being, and a sense of fulfillment that goes beyond mere academic success. It teaches you the invaluable skill of self-care, which you'll carry into every phase of your life, setting you up for long-term happiness and success.

Minimize Distractions

In a world that's always buzzing, beeping, and overflowing with information, finding a space to focus can feel like a Herculean task. Distractions are everywhere, especially when it comes to digital devices and the limitless universe of the internet. But, in order to truly flourish in school and beyond, mastering the art of minimizing distractions is essential.

First off, let's acknowledge that distractions aren't inherently evil. They become problematic when they start infringing on your time and mental space, hampering your productivity, creativity, and, ultimately, your fulfillment. Recognizing the need to reclaim your focus is the first step toward minimizing distractions.

Start by creating an environment that nurtures focus. Dedicate a quiet, clutter-free space for studying or working. This signals to your brain that it's time to get serious. Use headphones to block out noise if necessary, or consider playing some soft instrumental music if it helps you concentrate.

As for digital distractions, consider using apps that block or limit social media and other distractions during your study hours. Turn off notifications or set your devices on "Do Not Disturb" mode. Remember, every "ping" can yank your attention away from the task at hand.

Structuring your time can also be hugely beneficial. Try using techniques like the Pomodoro Technique, where you work for a set period (like 25 minutes), then take a short break (like 5 minutes), repeating this cycle a few times before taking a longer break (Cirillo, 2022). This strategy can help improve focus and productivity while preventing burnout.

It's also important to recognize when you need a break. Sometimes, our minds wander because they need rest. Taking short, regular breaks can actually increase your overall productivity and keep distractions at bay.

Finally, make mindfulness a habit. By training your mind to stay present and focused, you'll naturally become more resistant to distractions. This could be as simple as paying close attention to your breath for a few minutes each day, or you could explore more structured mindfulness practices like meditation or yoga.

Remember, the aim is not to eliminate all distractions; that's neither possible nor practical. The goal is to manage them effectively so they don't monopolize your time or mental space. In doing so, you'll not only boost your academic success, but you'll also pave the way for a deeper sense of fulfillment in all aspects of your life.

Eliminate Apathy and Find Direction

Apathy, a sense of indifference, a lack of interest or enthusiasm, can be like a thick fog that obscures our view of the future. It's a state that can creep up on anyone, particularly during our teen years when we're wrestling with so many changes and uncertainties. In our quest to find fulfillment, one critical step is to dissolve apathy and illuminate a clear direction forward.

The first step in dispelling apathy is recognizing its presence. Are you feeling unmotivated or indifferent toward your studies, hobbies, or relationships? Do you find it challenging to engage with your goals or dreams? If you nodded along, you might be grappling with apathy.

Next, let's remember that apathy isn't a personal failing; it's simply a sign that something needs attention. It could be rooted in fear, overwhelm, or a lack of self-confidence. Or, it could be a sign of burnout, a symptom of depression, or a side effect of chronic stress. If you're deeply struggling, reaching out to a trusted adult, counselor, or mental health professional is important.

To find your direction, start by rekindling your curiosity. Explore a range of subjects, hobbies, and activities without judgment or pressure. Allow yourself to experiment and discover what truly captures your interest. Remember, this is not about what you "should" do but about what sparks joy and engagement in you.

Setting personal goals can also provide a sense of direction. Your goals don't have to be grand or lofty. Start with small, achievable targets that align with your interests and values. Break down large goals into manageable steps, and celebrate each accomplishment, no matter how small. Seeing your progress can help stoke your motivation and dissolve apathy.

Creating a vision for your future can also give you a sense of direction. This isn't about mapping out every detail of your life. Instead, think of it as sketching a broad outline of where you want to go, who you want to be, and what you want to experience. Revisit and revise this vision as you grow and evolve; it's a guide, not a contract.

Finally, surround yourself with positive influences, people who inspire and encourage you. Seek out mentors, role models, or peers who are also driven by their passions and aspirations. Their energy and enthusiasm can be contagious, helping you overcome apathy and find your direction.

Finding fulfillment involves navigating through periods of apathy and uncertainty. But by kindling curiosity, setting personal goals, creating a vision for your future, and seeking out positive influences, you can banish apathy and shine a clear light on your path forward.

Drop Unhealthy Comparisons

Teenage years are marked by significant growth and self-discovery. It's a time when we begin to learn about our strengths, our interests, and our aspirations. But, this journey can often become muddled when we start comparing ourselves to others. In the pursuit of fulfillment, it's essential to drop unhealthy comparisons and embrace our unique path.

Comparisons, in essence, are not harmful. They can provide a sense of perspective, spark motivation, and encourage self-improvement. The danger lies in unhealthy comparisons, those that breed self-doubt, undermine our self-esteem, and distract us from our journey. We often forget that we're seeing a highlight reel of other's lives, not the behind-the-scenes struggles and hard work.

To drop unhealthy comparisons, start by fostering self-awareness. Identify the situations or people that trigger these negative comparisons. Are you scrolling through social media and feeling inadequate compared to your peers? Are you harshly comparing your academic performance with a classmate's?

Once you've identified these triggers, take proactive steps to counter them. If social media is a source of distress, consider limiting your screen time or curating your feed to include more inspiring and uplifting content. If academic comparisons are the problem, remind yourself that everyone has different strengths and learning styles. Your grades don't define your worth or predict your future success.

Next, focus on self-compassion. Remind yourself that everyone is unique, with their own set of strengths, challenges, and life experiences. Celebrate your achievements, however small they may seem. Be kind to yourself when you face setbacks or mistakes; they're a natural part of growth.

Also, direct your energy toward self-improvement rather than comparison. If you find yourself envying a peer's achievements, take a moment to consider what it is about their situation that you admire. Is it their dedication, their courage, or their skills? Instead of comparing, try to learn from them. What steps can you take to develop these qualities in yourself?

Lastly, cultivate gratitude. By focusing on the positive aspects of your life and the progress you've made, you can reduce feelings of inadequacy and envy. Keeping a gratitude journal can help reinforce this habit.

Dropping unhealthy comparisons is crucial for finding fulfillment. By fostering self-awareness, practicing self-compassion, focusing on self-improvement, and cultivating gratitude, you can shift your focus from comparison to self-growth and embrace your unique journey.

How Do I Become the Person I Want to Be?

The question of how to become the person you want to be is as old as time. It's a theme found in literature, spiritual texts, and philosophical musings throughout the ages. While there's no definitive roadmap, people have long searched for ways to realize their potential and live in alignment with their values.

This process of self-actualization often begins with knowing yourself deeply, your innate strengths, interests, and what drives you. Of course, relationships, finances, time management, goals, and habits all shape who we are and how we spend our days. It can take courage to assess these areas honestly and make changes where needed.

Growth is rarely linear. There are seasons of rapid progress and periods of plateau. With tenacity and the right systems of support, you can move past sticking points. In the end, becoming your best self is a lifelong endeavor. The effort comes with rich rewards, a sense of meaning, lasting contentment, and the ability to leave your unique stamp on the world.

This section explores principles and practices to guide you on the journey. While the path is different for everyone, you'll find tips to illuminate the way ahead. With an openness to learn and grow and compassion for yourself in the process, you can move step-by-step toward becoming the person you want to be.

Discover What Drives You

To become the person you want to be, it is essential to start by identifying what drives you and what makes you tick. Discovering your motivation can be a powerful tool to help you push past obstacles, keep going when things get tough, and make choices that align with your long-term goals.

In the realm of self-discovery, understanding what drives you involves deep self-reflection and introspection. What are the things that you are genuinely passionate about? What are the activities or tasks that you could do all day without feeling tired or bored? What are the causes that stir up your emotions and compel you to take action? The answers to these questions can provide crucial insights into your motivations and desires.

One practical approach to discovering your drivers is to keep a "passion journal." Every day, spend a few minutes jotting down the things that you loved doing, what made you feel accomplished, or what kept your mind engaged. Over time, you might start to see patterns and trends that point toward your deep-seated interests and motivations.

Another approach is to imagine your ideal future. Visualize what the best possible version of your life looks like in, say, five or ten years. What are you doing in this life? Who are you with? What achievements are you most proud of? This visualization exercise can help you identify the goals and aspirations that are most meaningful to you.

It's also important to remember that motivation isn't always about chasing grand ambitions or external rewards. Sometimes, the most potent drivers can be simple intrinsic motivations, like the joy of learning something new, the satisfaction of solving a difficult problem, or the fulfillment that comes from helping others.

In the journey of becoming the person you want to be, understanding what drives you acts as your compass. It can guide your decisions, help shape your goals, and fuel your perseverance. So embark on this quest of self-discovery, peel back the layers of your passions, desires, and interests, and uncover the powerful motivations that can propel you toward your true potential.

Understand Your Relationship With Money

As you pave your path toward becoming the person you want to be, understanding your relationship with money becomes an integral part of the journey. How you view and manage your finances can significantly impact your life choices, opportunities, and overall happiness. Whether it's about financial independence, giving back to society, or affording experiences you value, money often plays a crucial role in shaping your life.

To start with, it's important to examine your underlying beliefs and attitudes about money. Do you view it as a tool for freedom and opportunities, or do you associate it with stress and difficulties? Do you see it as a reward for hard work, or do you believe it's purely a matter of luck? Recognizing these underlying beliefs can help you understand your current financial behaviors and identify areas for potential change.

Next, consider your money habits. How do you typically handle your finances? Are you a saver or a spender? Do you budget your expenses or make impulsive purchases? Are you proactive in learning about financial management, or do you prefer to avoid thinking about it? By analyzing your habits, you can gain insights into your financial strengths and weaknesses.

One useful strategy to improve your relationship with money is to set clear financial goals. What do you want to achieve financially in the short term and long term? These could be things like saving for education, becoming debt-free, buying a home, or contributing to a cause you care about. Once you've set your goals, you can create a plan to achieve them, taking into account your income, expenses, and savings.

Also, remember that financial literacy is a crucial skill. It's never too early to learn about budgeting, investing, taxation, and retirement planning. The more you understand about these areas, the better equipped you'll be to make sound financial decisions.

Your relationship with money can significantly shape your path to becoming the person you want to be. By understanding your attitudes, improving your habits, setting clear goals, and boosting your financial literacy, you can harness the power of money to support your journey rather than letting it dictate your choices. Remember, money is a tool. How you use it is up to you.

Find Interests and Passions

Embarking on the journey to become the person you want to be is thrilling. However, sometimes, this voyage requires a compass, and finding your interests and passions could be the one you're looking for. Uncovering what truly excites you can illuminate your path, guiding you toward a fulfilling and enjoyable life.

Interests and passions often fuel motivation, breed curiosity, and inspire learning. When you're passionate about something, it no longer feels like a chore; instead, it becomes a source of joy, something you look forward to. This is the magic of pursuing what you genuinely love.

So, how do you find your interests and passions?

Begin by exploring. Try out new activities, read about different subjects, join clubs or societies, volunteer, or travel. You never know where you may find sparks of interest. Maybe it's the exhilaration of playing a musical instrument, the satisfaction of solving a complex equation, the serenity of painting, or the thrill of public speaking. The world is full of possibilities; your task is to tap into them.

Next, pay attention to your reactions. What activities make you lose track of time? What topics could you talk about for hours without getting bored? What dreams or goals excite you? Reflect on these questions. Often, your instinctive reactions and emotions can provide valuable clues about your passions.

Remember, it's okay if your interests evolve or change over time. You're not a static being. As you grow and experience life, your interests may shift, and that's perfectly normal. The key is to stay open and curious, continually seeking out and engaging with the things that bring you joy and fulfillment.

Finding your interests and passions doesn't happen overnight, but it's a journey worth embarking on. Not only can it lead you toward a more fulfilling life, but it can also help shape your identity, provide direction, and inspire growth.

Set Clear Goals

Imagine setting out on a journey with no clear destination in mind. The road may be full of exciting detours and scenic paths, but without a destination, the trip can quickly turn aimless and exhausting. In the quest to become the person you want to be, setting clear goals is akin to having a destination on your journey. Goals give your journey a sense of purpose and direction.

The act of setting clear and defined goals is a powerful tool for personal development. Goals serve as a roadmap, leading you through the maze of decisions and actions toward your desired self. By specifying what you want to achieve, you're setting clear markers for your journey, which can help keep you motivated and on track.

Here are some strategies to help you set clear goals:

SMART Goals: Make sure your goals are Specific, Measurable, Achievable, Relevant, and Time-bound. This structure can ensure your goals are well-defined and trackable (Mind Tools Content Team, 2022).

Write your goals down: The act of writing down your goals makes them tangible and serves as a constant reminder of what you're working toward.

Break down big goals into smaller tasks: Large, long-term goals can often feel overwhelming. Breaking them down into manageable, short-term tasks can make your goals feel more attainable and less daunting.

Visualize your goals: Create a vision board or use a journal to visualize your goals. This can make them feel more real and inspire you to work toward them.

Review and adjust your goals regularly: Goals aren't set in stone. As you progress on your journey, your aspirations might evolve. Regularly revisiting your goals allows you to make necessary adjustments and keeps your journey aligned with your evolving desires.

Remember, the process of setting goals isn't about creating a rigid plan that you must strictly adhere to. Instead, it's about providing direction and purpose to your efforts, thereby making your journey to becoming the person you want to be a more fulfilling and purposeful one.

Improve Time Management Skills

In the rush of life, time can feel like sand slipping through our fingers. Whether it's studying for exams, participating in extracurricular activities, spending time with loved ones, or simply taking a moment for self-care, juggling all these tasks can be daunting. The solution lies in enhancing our time management skills.

Improving your time management skills is not just about getting more tasks done; it's about focusing on what really matters to you, leading to increased productivity, reduced stress, and better quality of work, all essential ingredients on your journey to becoming the person you want to be.

Here are a few strategies to bolster your time management skills:

Prioritize your tasks: All tasks are not created equal. Some are essential to your goals, while others might be less important. Use tools like the Eisenhower Matrix to categorize your tasks into "Urgent," "Important," "Not Urgent," and "Not Important" to help identify what tasks need your immediate attention and what can be scheduled for later (Eisenhower, 2011).

Create a schedule: Planning your day can help you allot specific time slots for various tasks, reducing the chances of tasks eating into the time reserved for others. Remember to include breaks to avoid burnout.

Set realistic goals: Overestimating your capabilities can lead to disappointment and stress. Be honest with yourself about how much you can accomplish in a given time and set your goals accordingly.

Eliminate distractions: Identify what takes your attention away from your tasks and find ways to minimize these distractions when you're working or studying.

Use time management tools: There are various apps and tools available that can help you manage your time effectively. Find the one that works best for you and use it to keep track of your tasks and deadlines.

Practice mindfulness: Being present in the moment can significantly improve your efficiency. Mindfulness allows you to focus on the task at hand, improving the quality of your work and reducing the time it takes to complete it.

Time management is a journey of understanding your own pace, your priorities, and your working style. As you become better at managing your time, you'll find more space to grow into the person you aspire to be.

Learn to Say No

Navigating through life often involves juggling multiple responsibilities, interests, and demands from different corners. While it's admirable to be able to help others or to seize every opportunity, over-commitment can become a stumbling block on the path to becoming the person you aspire to be. This is where the power of saying "no" comes into play.

Saying "no" doesn't mean shutting out opportunities or being unhelpful. Instead, it's about understanding your capacity, respecting your priorities, and valuing your time. It's about creating healthy boundaries that allow you to focus on your personal growth.

Here are a few strategies to help you cultivate the ability to say "no":

Recognize your limits: Acknowledge that your time, energy, and resources are finite. You cannot possibly do everything, and that's okay.

Define your priorities: Understand what's most important to you in your journey to becoming the person you want to be. If a request doesn't align with these priorities or distracts you from them, it's okay to decline.

Consider the consequences: Before saying "yes" to a new commitment, consider its impact on your existing responsibilities and personal life. Are you ready to face the potential stress or overload?

Communicate effectively: If you need to decline a request, be honest and respectful in your response. You can express your appreciation for the offer or request, explain your reason for declining, and suggest alternatives if possible.

Practice self-compassion: Saying "no" can sometimes come with feelings of guilt or worry. Remember, choosing to prioritize yourself is not selfish; it's necessary for your well-being and personal growth.

Learning to say "no" might be challenging, especially if you're used to pleasing others or grabbing every opportunity. However, with time and practice, it becomes an empowering tool, helping you control your life's narrative and move closer to the person you aim to become.

Develop and Pursue Healthy Daily Habits

Becoming the person you want to be is often a result of the habits you develop and maintain daily. Like bricks to a building, each habit is a fundamental building block toward constructing the person you aspire to be. No matter how small, each habit plays an essential role, and collectively, they can lead to significant transformation.

Here are a few strategies to guide you in developing and pursuing healthy daily habits:

Start small: Aiming for radical change overnight might seem appealing, but it's often not sustainable. Instead, focus on small, manageable habits you can incorporate into your daily routine. The power of these small changes can be remarkable when compounded over time.

Create a routine: Habits thrive on consistency. Establish a daily routine that incorporates your new habits, be it morning meditation, a midday walk, or an evening gratitude journal.

Set clear intentions: Be explicit about what you want to achieve with your new habit. A clear purpose provides motivation and helps you focus on the desired outcome.

Implement habit triggers: Pair your new habit with an existing one. For instance, if you're trying to drink more water, tie it to brushing your teeth, and have a glass of water each time before or after brushing.

Reward progress: Celebrate your success along the way. The satisfaction derived from rewards serves as positive reinforcement, making the habit stick.

Practice patience and resilience: Habits take time to form and there might be days when you stumble. Instead of being disheartened, use these moments as learning experiences and keep going.

Healthy daily habits serve as the sturdy bedrock of personal growth. As you nurture these habits, you sow the seeds of discipline, perseverance, and transformation, inching closer every day to becoming the person you want to be.

Develop Systems for Studying and Learning

Learning is a lifelong journey, and the strategies we use to acquire new knowledge greatly influence the pace and depth of our learning. Developing effective systems for studying and learning can streamline this journey, making it more efficient, enjoyable, and fruitful.

Let's look at how you can create your unique learning system:

Identify your learning style: Do you learn best by reading, listening, observing, or doing? Once you recognize your preferred style—be it visual, auditory, reading/writing, or kinesthetic—you can tailor your study methods to suit your natural inclinations, leading to a more efficient learning process.

Establish a study schedule: Consistency is key in any learning process. Dedicate specific time blocks for focused studying each day. This establishes a routine, helping you to manage your time more effectively and avoid last-minute cramming.

Use active learning strategies: Active learning encourages your engagement with the material. This could be through summarizing information in your own words, teaching what you've learned to someone else, or applying your knowledge in real-world scenarios.

Break it down: Large amounts of information can be overwhelming. Breaking the content down into smaller, manageable chunks makes it easier to understand and remember. This technique, known as "chunking," is particularly useful when dealing with complex subjects.

Use tools and techniques: There are various tools and techniques designed to enhance learning. Mind maps help with understanding complex topics, flashcards assist in memorization, and digital apps can provide interactive learning experiences.

Review and reflect: Regularly review what you've learned to reinforce it in your memory. Additionally, take a moment to reflect on the learning process—what strategies worked? What didn't? This self-reflection helps you refine your learning system over time.

By cultivating your own learning system, you're not just optimizing your academic success; you're developing a crucial skill set for lifelong learning. This not only guides you on the path of becoming the person you want to be but also equips you to adapt to the constant flux of life.

Tenacity and Persistence

Tenacity and persistence are the fuel that powers your journey to becoming the person you want to be. They are the steady, unwavering resolve to keep moving forward, regardless of the challenges and setbacks you encounter along the way.

Define your "Why": The first step to cultivating tenacity and persistence is having a clear understanding of why your goals are important to you. This "why" becomes the anchor that keeps you grounded when things get tough.

Embrace the journey: Understand that the journey toward becoming who you want to be is not always going to be smooth sailing. There will be rough patches, detours, and even times when you might feel lost. Embrace these as part of the journey, knowing that they are shaping you into the person you aspire to be.

Adopt a growth mindset: See challenges as opportunities for growth rather than barriers to success. This shift in perspective allows you to approach difficulties with curiosity and resilience rather than fear or discouragement.

Break down goals: Large goals can feel overwhelming and unachievable, leading to a loss of motivation. Breaking them down into smaller, manageable tasks can make the process seem less daunting, making it easier for you to keep moving forward.

Celebrate small wins: Celebrating small victories along the way boosts your motivation and reaffirms your ability to reach your larger goals. Each step forward, no matter how small, is a testament to your tenacity.

Seek support: Surround yourself with supportive individuals who believe in your abilities and cheer you on. Their positive reinforcement can invigorate your resolve when you need it the most.

Practice self-care: It's essential to take care of your physical, mental, and emotional health during this journey. This ensures you have the energy and mindset to persist, even during challenging times.

Inculcating tenacity and persistence isn't about never falling but rising each time you fall. It's about continually pushing your boundaries, overcoming hurdles, and relentlessly pursuing your ambitions. Remember, the person you want to be is molded not just by their achievements but by their grit and resilience in the face of adversity.

Recognize That Life Has Seasons

Just as the earth has its seasons, so too does life. Recognizing this can empower you to navigate the ebbs and flows of your journey to becoming the person you want to be.

Acknowledge the seasons: Life consists of various seasons, periods of growth and bloom, times of rest and recovery, and even moments of harsh, cold change. Recognizing and accepting these seasons as natural parts of your journey can help you respond more effectively to the shifting dynamics of life.

Respect each season: Every season in life holds value. The "summer" season might be filled with productivity, achievement, and joy, while the "winter" season might bring challenges, introspection, and growth through adversity. Respect the purpose each season serves in your development.

Be flexible and adaptive: Understand that each season requires a different response. There may be times when you need to push hard toward your goals, and there may be times when it's better to slow down, reflect, and recharge. Being flexible and adaptive enables you to harness the power of each season effectively.

Recognize seasonal transitions: Change often doesn't happen overnight. There's usually a period of transition, where elements of the past season mix with hints of the upcoming one. Recognize these transitional periods, and prepare yourself for the change.

Practice self-compassion: Some seasons are harder than others, and it's crucial to practice self-compassion during these challenging times. Remember, it's okay to stumble and fall. What matters most is your willingness to get up, dust off, and keep moving forward.

Celebrate seasonal successes: Each season will bring its own set of victories and achievements, no matter how small they may seem. Celebrate these wins as signs of your ongoing growth and progress.

By recognizing that life has seasons, you learn to appreciate the cyclical nature of growth and development. This understanding will help you remain patient, resilient, and hopeful as you continue to evolve into the person you aspire to be. After all, spring always follows winter, bringing with it new life, growth, and opportunities.

Succeeding in School and Beyond—A Comprehensive Approach

Materials needed: A journal or notebook, a pen, some quiet time, and a commitment to personal growth.

Time required: About 1 hour per day, although this can be divided into smaller segments throughout the day.

Instructions: Schedule time each day to address one of the prompts below until you have considered, reflected on, and responded to each prompt.

Identify your motivation: Write down what truly motivates you. It could be a personal goal, an aspiration, or even a person. Keep this at the forefront of your mind as you navigate through school and beyond.

Acknowledge your anxiety: Record moments when you feel anxious. Note down the triggers and how you respond to them. Over time, try to implement stress management techniques to handle these situations.

Understand your personality: Write down your strengths, weaknesses, interests, and disinterests. Use this understanding to leverage your strengths and work on your weaknesses.

Manage stress and fatigue: Designate time every day for relaxation and rejuvenation. This could be in the form of reading, listening to music, practicing yoga, or even a power nap.

Minimize distractions: Identify things or situations that often distract you from your work or study. Try to eliminate these distractions or set a schedule when you can indulge in them without affecting your productivity.

Combat apathy and find direction: Write about times you felt indifferent or lacked direction. Try to understand why it happened and how you can infuse more passion and purpose into your life.

Drop unhealthy comparisons: Be conscious of moments when you compare yourself with others. Write down your feelings during these moments and gradually learn to celebrate your unique journey.

Discover what drives you: Reflect on moments you've felt highly motivated and driven. What common factors can you identify? How can you recreate these conditions in your everyday life?

Understand your relationship with money: Write down your thoughts and feelings about money. Are they mostly positive, negative, or neutral? This can help you develop a healthier and more productive attitude toward money.

Find your interests and passions: Write about activities or topics that genuinely excite you. This can guide you toward a career or life path that you will find fulfilling and enjoyable.

Set clear goals: Write down your short-term and long-term goals. Make them specific, measurable, achievable, relevant, and time-bound (SMART).

Improve time management: Keep a log of how you spend your time for a week. Identify areas where you can save time and areas you need to devote more time to.

Learn to say no: Practice saying "no" to tasks or activities that don't align with your goals or values. It's essential to prioritize your time and energy.

Healthy daily habits: Create a list of healthy habits you would like to incorporate into your daily routine. Start small and gradually build on them.

Develop systems for studying and learning: Try different studying and learning techniques to see what works best for you. Implement these methods into your regular study routine.

Tenacity and persistence: Reflect on a time you overcame a challenging situation through persistence. Use this as a reminder of your ability to persevere when faced with difficulties.

Recognize that life has seasons: Understand that life is a series of seasons, each with its own set of challenges and opportunities. Write down what you're learning in your current "season."

Remember, this is a journey of self-discovery and growth. Be patient with yourself and celebrate your small victories along the way!

Conclusion

What a journey we've been on! Reading this book has been like setting out on a grand adventure, exploring the wild and wonderful terrain of our inner selves.

Think back to when we first started. We were digging deep into motivation and discovering how to ignite that inner fire. Remember all those practical tools like the "Buddy System" and "Vision Boards"? They made those lofty ideas feel real and attainable, didn't they?

Then, we tackled some tough stuff. Anxiety, stress, understanding our unique personalities—it was all about shining a light on the shadowy corners of ourselves. We learned that recognizing our own strengths and quirks is the first step toward growth. That's powerful stuff.

One chapter that really hit home was about fulfillment. It's such a personal, fluid thing, and there's no perfect formula. But, this book gave us some guidance to start carving our own paths toward it.

And how about that monumental question: "How Do I Become the Person I Want to Be?" We've been on a wild ride figuring that one out. Identifying our passions, setting goals, learning when to say "no," and realizing the importance of persisting, it's been transformative.

But here's the thing, we're not done yet. This isn't the end of our journey; it's just the beginning. Every insight and lesson we've gathered is a seed waiting to be planted, nurtured, and cultivated.

Yes, change can be unsettling, but it's also the birthplace of growth. So, let's embrace the discomfort and keep pushing forward.

Let's also remember to enjoy the ride. Sure, we've got our eyes on the prize, but life's magic happens in the "now." Each moment, each victory, and yes, even each setback, they're all stepping stones on our unique path.

The end of this book? It's not really an end. It's the start of a whole new adventure—an adventure where you're the hero, shaping your own story.

And remember, you're not alone. There's a whole tribe of us, dreamers and doers, all navigating this winding road of personal growth together.

So, here's to the journey so far and the journey still to come. Let's keep asking, seeking, learning, and growing. There's a world of potential out there waiting for us to tap into it. And there's a world of potential within us, just itching to be unleashed. Whenever you need a reminder, revisit the sections of the book that make sense; these strategies are useful at different stages of your life and are worth returning to.

Onwards and upwards, my friend. The road is waiting. Let's keep moving, keep exploring, keep evolving. The best is yet to come!

References

Ames, D. R., Lee, A. J., & Wazlawek, A. S. (2017). Interpersonal assertiveness: Inside the balancing act. *Social and personality psychology compass, 11*(8), e12317.

Anda, R.F., Whitfield, C.L., Felitti, V.J., Chapman, D., Edwards, V.J., Dube, S.R., & Williamson, D.F. (2002). Adverse childhood experiences, alcoholic parents, and later risk of alcoholism and depression. *Psychiatric services, 53*(8), 1001-1009.

Anthony Rapp quotes. (n.d.). BrainyQuote.com. Web site: https://www.brainyquote.com/quotes/anthony_rapp_128808

Bandura, A. (1997). *Self-efficacy: The exercise of control.* New York: W.H. Freeman.

Bandura, A. (1986). The explanatory and predictive scope of self-efficacy theory. *Journal of social and clinical psychology, 4*(3), 359-373.

Baumeister, R.F., Campbell, J.D., Krueger, J.I., & Vohs, K.D. (2003). Does High Self-Esteem Cause Better Performance, Interpersonal Success, Happiness, or Healthier Lifestyles? *Psychological Science in the Public Interest, 4*(1), 1–44.

Beck, A. T. (1967). *Depression: Clinical, experimental, and theoretical aspects.* Harper & Row.

Beck, J. S. (2011). *Cognitive behavior therapy, basics and beyond* (2nd ed.). Guilford Press.

Burns, D. D. (1980). The perfectionist's script for self-defeat. *Psychology today, 14*(6), 34–52.

Branden, N. (1994). *Six pillars of self-esteem.* Bantam.

Briggs, K. C. (1987). *Myers-Briggs type indicator.* Palo Alto, Calif. Consulting Psychologists Press.

Carver, C. S. (1998). Resilience and thriving: Issues, models, and linkages. *Journal of social issues, 54*(2), 245-266.

Cirillo, F. (2022). *The Pomodoro® Technique Book* | Cirillo Consulting GmbH. Francescocirillo.com. https://francescocirillo.com/products/the-pomodoro-technique

Cooley, C. H. (1902). *Human nature and the social order.* Scribner's.

Crocker, J., & Wolfe, C. T. (2001). Contingencies of self-worth. *Psychological review, 108*(3), 593.

Donnellan, M. B., Trzesniewski, K. H., Robins, R. W., Moffitt, T. E., & Caspi, A. (2005). Low self-esteem is related to aggression, antisocial behavior, and delinquency. *Psychological science, 16*(4), 328–335.

Downey, G., Freitas, A. L., Michaelis, B., & Khouri, H. (1998). The self-fulfilling prophecy in close relationships: rejection sensitivity and rejection by romantic partners. *Journal of personality and social psychology, 75*(2), 545–560. https://doi.org/10.1037//0022-3514.75.2.545

Eisenhower. (2011). *The Eisenhower Matrix.* Eisenhower. https://www.eisenhower.me/eisenhower-matrix/

Flett, G. L., Hewitt, P. L., Besser, A., Su, C., Vaillancourt, T., Boucher, D., Munro, Y., & Davidson, L. A. (2002). Perfectionism, belief in the perfectibility of people, and interpersonal problems. *Journal of Psychopathology and Behavioral Assessment, 24*(4), 279-291.

Frost, R. O., Marten, P., Lahart, C., & Rosenblate, R. (1990). The dimensions of perfectionism. *Cognitive therapy and research, 14*(5), 449-468.

Gilbert, R., Widom, C. S., Browne, K., Fergusson, D., Webb, E., & Janson, S. (2009). Burden and consequences of child maltreatment in high-income countries. *The Lancet, 373*(9657), 68–81. https://doi.org/10.1016/s0140-6736(08)61706-7

Girodo, M., Dotzenroth, S. E., & Stein, S. J. (1981). Causal attribution bias in shy males: Implications for self-esteem and self-confidence. *Cognitive therapy and research, 5*(4), 325–338.

Grogan, S. (2008). *Body Image: Understanding Body Dissatisfaction in Men, Women and Children.* Routledge.

Harter, S. (1999). *The construction of the self: A developmental perspective.* Guilford Press.

Heppner, P. P., & Heppner, M. J. (2004). *Writing and publishing your thesis, dissertation & research: A guide for students in the helping professions.* Brooks/Cole.

Hewitt, P. L., & Flett, G. L. (2003). Dimensions of perfectionism, daily stress, and depression: A test of the specific vulnerability hypothesis. *Journal of abnormal psychology, 112*(1), 4-12.

Joiner, T. E., & Metalsky, G. I. (2001). Excessive reassurance seeking: Delineating a risk factor involved in the development of depressive symptoms. *Psychological science, 12*(5), 371–378.

Kaplan, A., & Maehr, M. L. (1999). Achievement goals and student well-being. *Contemporary Educational Psychology, 24*(4), 330-358.

Kidd, S., & Shahar, G. (2008). Resilience in homeless youth: The key role of self-esteem. *American journal of orthopsychiatry, 78*(2), 163–172. https://doi.org/10.1037/0002-9432.78.2.163

Kumar, S., & Mishra, A. (2011). Work life balance and job satisfaction among the working women of banking and education sector–a comparative study. *International journal of advancements in research & technology, 1*(2), 23-29.

Lange, A., & Jakubowski, P. (1976). *Responsible assertive behavior: Cognitive/behavioral procedures for trainers.* Research Press

Leary, M. R. (1990). Responses to Social Exclusion: Social Anxiety, Jealousy, Loneliness, Depression, and Low Self-Esteem. Journal of Social and Clinical Psychology, 9(2), 221–229. https://doi.org/10.1521/jscp.1990.9.2.221

Leary, M. R., Tambor, E. S., Terdal, S. K., & Downs, D. L. (1995). Self-esteem as an interpersonal monitor: The sociometer hypothesis. *Journal of personality and social psychology, 68*(3), 518.

Locke, E. A., Frederick, E., Lee, C., & Bobko, P. (1984). Effect of self-efficacy, goals, and task strategies on task performance. *Journal of applied psychology, 69*(2), 241.

Lutz, A., Slagter, H. A., Dunne, J. D., & Davidson, R. J. (2008). Attention regulation and monitoring in meditation. *Trends in cognitive sciences, 12*(4), 163-169

Mann, M., Hosman, C. M. H., Schaalma, H. P., & De Vries, N. K. (2004). Self-esteem in a broad-spectrum approach for mental health promotion. *Health education research, 19*(4), 357-372.

Martin, A. J., Nejad, H. G., Colmar, S., & Liem, G. A. (2012). Adaptability: Conceptual and empirical perspectives on responses to change, novelty and uncertainty. *Australian Journal of Guidance and Counselling, 22*(1), 58-81.

Maslow, A. H. (1943). A theory of human motivation. *Psychological Review, 50*(4), 370.

Masten, A. S. (2001). Ordinary magic: Resilience processes in development. *American Psychologist, 56*(3), 227.

McCrae, R. R., & Costa, P. T. (1987). Validation of the five-factor model of personality across instruments and observers. *Journal of personality and social psychology, 52*(1), 81.

McGee, R., & Williams, S. (2000). Does low self-esteem predict health compromising behaviours among adolescents? *Journal of adolescence, 23*(5), 569–582. https://doi.org/10.1006/jado.2000.0344

Mind Tools Content Team. (2022). *SMART Goals*. Mind Tools. https://www.mindtools.com/a4wo118/smart-goals

Murray, S. L., Holmes, J. G., Griffin, D. W., Bellavia, G., & Rose, P. (2001). The Mismeasure of Love: How Self-Doubt Contaminates Relationship Beliefs. *Personality and social psychology bulletin, 27*(4), 423–436. https://doi.org/10.1177/0146167201274004

Murray, S. L., Holmes, J. G., & Collins, N. L. (2006). Optimizing assurance: The risk regulation system in relationships. *Psychological bulletin, 132*(5), 641.

Neff, K. D. (2003). The Development and Validation of a Scale to Measure Self-Compassion. *Self and identity, 2*(3), 223–250.

Neff, K. D. (2011). Self-compassion, self-esteem, and well-being. *Social and personality psychology compass, 5*(1), 1-12.

Neff, K. D., & Vonk, R. (2009). Self-compassion versus global self-esteem: two different ways of relating to oneself. *Journal of personality, 77*(1), 23-50.

Nosek, M.A., Hughes, R.B., Swedlund, N., Taylor, H.B., & Swank, P. (2003). Self-esteem and women with disabilities. *Social science & medicine, 56*(8), 1737-1747.

Orth, U., Robins, R. W., & Meier, L. L. (2009). Disentangling the effects of low self-esteem and stressful events on depression: findings from three longitudinal studies. *Journal of personality and social psychology, 97*(2), 307–321. https://doi.org/10.1037/a0015645

Orth, U., Robins, R. W., & Widaman, K. F. (2012). Life-span development of self-esteem and its effects on important life outcomes. *Journal of personality and social psychology, 102*(6), 1271.

Orth, U., Robins, R. W., & Roberts, B. W. (2008). Low self-esteem prospectively predicts depression in adolescence and young adulthood. *Journal of personality and social psychology, 95*(3), 695.

Orth, U., & Robins, R. W. (2013). Understanding the link between low self-esteem and depression. *Current directions in psychological science, 22*(6), 455-460.

Orson Welles quotes. (n.d.). BrainyQuote.com. https://www.brainyquote.com/quotes/orson_welles_142014

Pierce, T., Sarason, I. G., & Sarason, B. R. (1996). General and relationship-based perceptions of social support: are two constructs better than one? *Journal of personality and social psychology, 71*(6), 1029

Purpose Of Life Quotes (645 quotes). (2010). Goodreads.com. https://www.goodreads.com/quotes/tag/purpose-of-life

Reis, H. T., Collins, W. A., & Berscheid, E. (2000). The relationship context of human behavior and development. *Psychological bulletin, 126*(6), 844.

Reijntjes, A., Kamphuis, J.H., Prinzie, P., & Telch, M.J. (2010). Peer victimization and internalizing problems in children: A meta-analysis of longitudinal studies. *Child abuse & neglect, 34*(4), 244-252.

Roberts, B. W., & Monroe, S. M. (1992). Vulnerable self-esteem and depressive symptoms: Prospective findings comparing three alternative conceptualizations. *Journal of personality and social psychology, 62*(5), 804–812.

Rodriguez, L. M., Litt, D. M., & Stewart, S. H. (2016). *Drinking to cope with the negative consequences of conformity drinking motives: An exploratory investigation. Addictive behaviors, 53*, 180-187.

Rodriguez, M. L., & Kelly, A. E. (2006). Health effects of disclosing secrets to imagined accepting versus nonaccepting confidants. *Journal of social and clinical psychology, 25*(9), 1023–1047.

Rosenberg, M. (1965). *Society and the adolescent self-image.* Princeton University Press.

Rubin, K. H., Dwyer, K. M., Booth-LaForce, C., Kim, A. H., Burgess, K. B., & Rose-Krasnor, L. (2004). Attachment, friendship, and psychosocial functioning in early adolescence. *The journal of early adolescence, 24*(4), 326-356.

Rüsch, N., Lieb, K., Göttler, I., Hermann, C., Schramm, E., Richter, H., ... & Bohus, M. (2007). Shame and implicit self-concept in women with borderline personality disorder. *American journal of psychiatry, 164*(3), 500-508.

Schwartz, S. J., Côté, J. E., & Arnett, J. J. (2005). Identity and agency in emerging adulthood: Two developmental routes in the individualization process. *Youth & Society, 37*(2), 201–229.

Srivastava, K., & Kumar, R. (2017). Occupational stress and job satisfaction among doctors: A cross-sectional study in North India. *Delhi Psychiatry Journal, 20*(1), 14.

Sowislo, J.F., & Orth, U. (2013). Does low self-esteem predict depression and anxiety? A meta-analysis of longitudinal studies. *Psychological bulletin, 139*(1), 213.

Thoma, S. J., & Dong, Y. (2014). The Defining Issues Test of moral judgment development. *Behavioral development, 18*(3), 219-241.

Trzesniewski, K.H., Donnellan, M.B., Moffitt, T.E., Robins, R.W., Poulton, R., & Caspi, A. (2006). Low self-esteem during adolescence predicts poor health, criminal behavior, and limited economic prospects during adulthood. *Developmental psychology, 42*(2), 381.

Wayne Dyer quotes. (n.d.). BrainyQuote.com. https://www.brainyquote.com/quotes/wayne_dyer_154414

www.ingramcontent.com/pod-product-compliance
Lightning Source LLC
LaVergne TN
LVHW051601080426
835510LV00020B/3084